Endorsement

This slender book is a rare gift: a dis[tillation of the] most profound insights that the ever-[......... Richard] Barrett has accumulated over decades of path-breaking work. If every individual and organisation used Richard's frameworks to guide their actions, our world would be a blessed place.

Raj Sisodia, *FW Olin Distinguished Professor of Global Business, Babson College Co-founder & Chairman Emeritus, Conscious Capitalism Inc., USA.*

The best book on values I have ever read. Richard Barrett is one of the world's foremost experts on the subject; nevertheless he manages to inhabit the 'beginner's mind': He takes us back to the fundamental truths about the importance of values in our personal, organisational and societal lives.

Ruth Steinholtz, *Founder and Managing Partner of AretéWork LLP, UK.*

The depth of wisdom and research that has gone into Richard's powerful new book is truly inspirational and potentially world-changing. It gives us the ability to have an in-depth understanding of not only our own worldviews and why they are as they are, but also of those of the full spectrum of humanity. Imagine what our world will be like when every human being has this level of awareness. This book creates the possibility.

Kate Stephenson, *Managing Director Illuminesta, UK.*

An invaluable point of reference for anyone seeking a deeper understanding of human values and consciousness evolution! Packed with the most condensed knowledge and wisdom, this book is simple yet elegant, accessible yet profound, vast in scope yet robust in application, reflecting the author's soulful balance of human spirit and engineering precision.

Niran Jiang, *Co-founder and Director, Institute of Human Excellence, Australia.*

Imagine a master appearing before you, to enlighten you ... meet Richard Barrett and his book Everything I Have Learned about Values. A must-read for all awakening souls.

Lawrence Ford, *Shaman of Wall Street & CEO of Conscious Capital Wealth Management, USA.*

Guru on values and philosopher Richard Barrett presents a concise overview of values and their importance to personal, organisational and societal development. *Everything I Have Learned About Values* is a must read for everyone.

Patrik Andersson, *CEO & Chairman Values Academy, Sweden.*

In this slim volume, Richard Barrett summarises his decades of research and reflection on human values, providing a provocative framework for viewing, understanding and perhaps most importantly, influencing individual, organisational and societal experience. By inviting us to ask new questions about our own choices, as people and nations, Barrett gently leads us to see a potential for transformative, and sorely needed, new answers.

Mary C. Gentile Ph.D, *University of Virginia Darden School of Business, USA.*

This is the book I have been wishing Richard Barrett would write. It's the call to action the world needs right now! I have read most of his work and this one beautifully integrates and offers you the essence of "What values are all about". *Everything I Have Learned About Values* is a must for all leaders who want to make a difference and a lasting changes to their lives. It's a quick and very profound read that will help you make sense of how transformation happens through the expansion of human consciousness, from the individual level, the organisational level, all the way through to the national level. Richard masterfully distills very complex ideas in very simple and clear, easy to understand language, illustrating it with real life examples from his personal experiences and observations. The work is grounded in research and an ever-growing database of results from the Barrett Values Centre's values assessments used by leaders, organisations, communities and nations all over the world.

Ina Gjikondi-Cecchetto, *Director, Executive Education & Leadership Coaching Services, Center for Excellence in Public Leadership, The George Washington University, USA.*

Richard Barrett lays out a clear path on how to use values to transform yourself, your organisations and society. I have used Richard's research in my work for more than 10 years and this book is an essential read for transformation agents as well as senior executives.

Stephane Leblanc, *CEO, International Centre for Conscious Leadership, Canada.*

This book is a perfect introduction for anyone interested in working with values in any walk of life. Richard Barrett shares everything he has discovered about the fundamental principles of human well-being.

Patrik Somers-Stephenson, *Values Consultant andEvolutionary Coaching Facilitator, Evolution Inside Out Ltd.*

Richard Barrett's book provides the perfect introduction to the subject of values. In an easy and rewarding style, he successfully combines his deep knowledge with his most important learnings to clearly articulate why we need more conscious values-led leadership in the world.

Graham Massey, *Co-founder of The House (Purpose-led brand, leadership and culture consultancy), UK.*

An astoundingly succinct tour through understanding values at the personal, organisational and societal level, underpinned throughout by some fascinating data. All in one place and readable in one sitting! I highly recommend to anyone wanting to build a values-driven life, organisation or society.

Liz Murphy, *UK Values Alliance Steering Group.*

Richard Barrett hits the nail right on the head. He brings his immense values knowledge across in a concise and understandable way. It's incredible what I have got out of this book as an individual, as an entrepreneur and as a member of my society.

Dr. Andrea Maria Bokler,
Change Management, Germany.

I truly believe in Richard's work. His wealth of knowledge in personal, organisational and societal transformation has captivated and inspired me for close to two decades. Richard has used his model to develop a consciousness indicator for nations that in my experience will make the transformation of our global society possible. *Everything I Have Learned About Values* is an insightful and easy to follow introduction into Richard's life's work and a significant contribution to building a better world.

Annalise Jennings,
Director – Dynamic Exchange, Australia.

Everything I Have Learned About Values is required reading for anyone currently in, or aspiring to be in a leadership role and interested in increasing their values literacy. Richard's comprehensive overview demonstrates how values underpin everything we do, and how understanding the Seven Levels of Consciousness model is the key to transforming individuals and organisations on global scale.

Kathleen Seeley, *Founder/President, Massively Human Leadership™, Canada.*

Having worked significantly with Richard Barrett's Seven Levels of Consciousness and its many rich applications, in particular, bringing awareness to values based living and leadership, this is a wonderful collation of his deep understanding of our human needs, motivations and consciousness and a great resource for helping to deepen the understanding and application of values in our world today.

Mike Budden, *Managing Partner, Barry-Wehmiller Leadership Institute, South Africa.*

I highly recommend Richard Barrett's latest book, *Everything I Have Learned About Values.* Richard is a friend, colleague and arguably the world's leading expert on values and culture transformation. In this quick and inspirational read, Richard pulls together his life's work and provides an advanced education in his "Seven Levels of Consciousness Model". He demonstrates how values serve as a tool for understanding human motivation. He also demonstrates how this understanding can be utilised for individual, organisational and societal transformation to serve humanity in a positive way.

Jack Canfield, Co-author, *The Success Principles: How to Get From Where You Are to Where You Want to Be*™, **USA.**

From the first page, I loved the whole concept. Writing a book a person could read in a few hours, to absorb what has taken Richard a lifetime to learn. *Everything I Have Learned About Values* provides new insights and ways of relating to values which I believe will reinforce the importance of values to leaders in a deeply profound way.

Joanna Barclay,
CEO, Culture Leadership Group, Singapore.

Richard and his team at the Barrett Values Centre have been instrumental in contributing towards how culture impacts high performance organisations. This is a must-read book for all who are passionate about values-driven organisations and is a great resource to help translate a seemingly fuzzy concept of organisation culture to something practical, measurable and implementable. Our clients from public, private and not-for-profit sectors have benefitted greatly from the use of BVC's Culture Transformation Tools and we are blessed to be part of this very meaningful and impactful journey with them.

Vincent Ho, *Director, aAdvantage Consulting Group Pte Ltd, Singapore.*

Richard Barrett's enlightening mind leads us into the ultimate trip: navigating inside your own DNA hologram, up and down each helix of your values (personal, social, national), understanding how they intertwine (why you did what you did, or didn't) and, by unscrambling and realigning your value strands, how to create what you value most now.

Daniel Quirici, *Echo Capital, UK.*

In this new book Richard is condensing in a few pages all he has learned about values through three different perspectives: personal, organisational and societal. If you are just a beginner or a student of his framework of human consciousness, I recommend this book wholeheartedly.

Roberto Ziemer,
Sócio/Fundador da Liderança Integral, Brazil.

Based on twenty years of deep engagement with values and consciousness, Richard Barrett brings lightness and clarity to the topic, making it understandable for everyone, practitioners and newcomers alike. I very much like the way it weaves his own life experiences into his writings. I commend this book to everyone who is interested in getting a foundation understanding of values.

Pleuntje van Meer,
Synnova, Founding Partner, The Netherlands.

I am so grateful that Richard and his colleague, Bjorn, had the conversation that resulted essentially in a primer about human values based on all of Richard's books. It is lovely to have all of the highlights in one place. Knowing that Richard receives downloads with regard to his books, perhaps it would be more accurate to call this a primer of Richard's soul and I am glad we are the lucky recipients!

B. Ann Dinan Ph.D, M.S.S.A.,
C.P.C.C., President, Deeper Leadership Institute, USA.

Everything I have Learned about Values is the only short book I know written in an accessible way to describe what everyone would benefit to understand about human development and how we make sense and meaning in life and work. I recommend this book to anyone with an open mind and an interest in how we can flourish and grow as individuals and as a society.

Martin Egan, *(PhD, MBACP Accred, FRSA) Psychotherapist and Organizational Culture Consultant, UK.*

Books by Richard Barrett

The Values-Driven Organization: Cultural Health and Employee Well-Being as a Pathway to Sustainable Performance (2017)

A New Psychology of Human Well-Being: An Exploration of the Influence of Ego-Soul Dynamics on Mental and Physical Health (2016)

The Metrics of Human Consciousness (2015)

Evolutionary Coaching: A Values-Based Approach to Unleashing Human Potential (2014)

The Values-Driven Organization: Unleashing Human Potential for Performance and Profit (2013)

What My Soul Told Me: A Practical Guide to Soul Activation (2012)

Love, Fear and the Destiny of Nations: The Impact of the Evolution of Human Consciousness on World Affairs (2011)

The New Leadership Paradigm (2010)

Building a Values-Driven Organization: A Whole System Approach to Cultural Transformation (2006)

Liberating the Corporate Soul: Building a Visionary Organization (1998)

A Guide to Liberating Your Soul (1995)

EVERYTHING
I HAVE LEARNED
ABOUT VALUES

RICHARD BARRETT

Copyright © 2018 Richard Barrett.

All rights reserved. No part of this book may be reproduced, stored, or transmitted by any means—whether auditory, graphic, mechanical, or electronic—without written permission of the author, except in the case of brief excerpts used in critical articles and reviews. Unauthorized reproduction of any part of this work is illegal and is punishable by law.

This book is a work of non-fiction. Unless otherwise noted, the author and the publisher make no explicit guarantees as to the accuracy of the information contained in this book and in some cases, names of people and places have been altered to protect their privacy.

Barrett Values Centre, Cultural Transformation Tools, Cultural Entropy, Seven Levels of Consciousness, Seven Stages of Psychological Development and Full-Spectrum Consciousness are registered trademarks of Barrett Values Centre LLC.

ISBN: 978-1-4834-7941-5 (sc)
ISBN: 978-1-4834-7940-8 (e)

Because of the dynamic nature of the Internet, any web addresses or links contained in this book may have changed since publication and may no longer be valid. The views expressed in this work are solely those of the author and do not necessarily reflect the views of the publisher, and the publisher hereby disclaims any responsibility for them.

Any people depicted in stock imagery provided by Thinkstock are models, and such images are being used for illustrative purposes only.
Certain stock imagery © Thinkstock.

Lulu Publishing Services rev. date: 01/30/2018

Dedication

This book is dedicated to all those who aspire to live a values-driven life.

Table of Contents

Foreword xix
Preface xxi

Chapter 1: Introduction 1
Chapter 2: Everything I have learned about values
               in my personal life 11
Chapter 3: Everything I have learned about values
               in my organizational life 37
Chapter 4: Everything I have learned about values
               in my societal life 53

Epilogue 101
Annex 1: The formation of Hitler's personality 103
Annex 2: The formation of Gandhi's personality 107
Index 111

List of Figures

Figure 1.1: Top ten values of 500,000 people 3
Figure 2.1: My top ten values 12
Figure 3.1: Values plot for a low-performance organization 42
Figure 3.2: Values plot for a high-performance organization 45
Figure 3.3: Values associated with high and low personal entropy 48
Figure 4.1: HI rankings vs. GCI rankings 83
Figure 4.2: GF rankings vs. GCI rankings 84
Figure 4.3: Values plot for Iceland (2008) 89
Figure 4.4: Values plot for the UAE (2012) 90

List of Tables

Table 2.1: The tasks and needs associate with the seven stages of psychological development 26
Table 2.2: Concerns and feelings associated with the mastery of each stage of development 27
Table 2.3: The positive and limiting values associated with the seven levels of personal consciousness 29
Table 3.1: Value jumps for a low-performance organization 43
Table 3.2: Value jumps for a high-performance organization 46
Table 4.1: Levels of identity/awareness and focus of worldviews 55
Table 4.2: Correspondence between Levels of identity/awareness and individual stages of psychological development 57
Table 4.3: Levels of identity/awareness (worldviews) and Cultural Entropy scores in 25 nations 87
Table 4.4: Value jumps for Iceland (2008) 89
Table 4.5: Value jumps for the UAE (2012) 91
Table 4.6: Cultural Entropy scores for France (2012 – 2016) 94
Table 4.7: Cultural Entropy scores for Sweden (2009 – 2017) 95

Foreword

NOVEMBER, 2016, STOCKHOLM, SWEDEN: HAVING dinner with Richard Barrett—by many considered the world's leading expert on human values—in a quiet restaurant, after one of his seminars.

"What was your take away?" Richard asks with his characteristic curious smile. "It struck me," I said, "Since values are the basic operating system for the human being, or as you put it, *the energetic drivers of our aspirations and intentions* "you are sitting on *the source code* of human motivation."

Richard nods enthusiastically, and with a quizzical look on his face, asks me: "What should I do with all this information and knowledge? I would like everyone to benefit from what I have discovered about the fundamental principles of human well-being."

"Your challenge," I say, "Is perhaps no different to any other thought-leader who has spent decades researching a particular subject. You simply know too much! The question you have to address, I think, is how do you package all this knowledge?"

"I know, I know" Richard responds, "What would be your advice?"

"I always seek inspiration from the quote of T.S. Elliot" I replied:

"We shall not cease from exploration, and the end of all our exploring will be to arrive where we started and know the place for the first time."

"In other words" I add, "Why not revisit the starting-point of your work as if it was the first time and write an introductory book on everything you've learned about the role of values in the lives of individuals, organizations and society? Stick to your most important findings. Make it a book that people can read in a few hours. Afterwards, they can always go to your other books to learn more."

"That's it!" Richard responded gleefully, "I'd never thought of that. That's what I need to do." After a long and thoughtful moment, he asks me "Will you write the Foreword?"

"With pleasure" I responded. "I strongly believe that people will benefit from being introduced to your powerful insights and especially the Seven Stages of Psychological Development Model. I have found it very illuminating. It has helped me understand people in a very different way."

***

In July 2017, I read the final manuscript of *Everything I have learned about values*. I believe it is an indispensable introduction to Richard Barrett's life-long work on human values. It not only helps you to become aware of the significant role values play in your life, it also helps you better understand every stage of your life's journey, and this is what I believe makes the book profoundly transformative at a personal level.

Richard's insights into organizational development are equally profound. He constantly reminds me: "Organizations don't transform. People do." In other words, organizational transformation begins with the personal transformation of the leaders. What he has done at the Barrett Values Centre is to make the intangibles, tangible. He has created ways of measuring what truly matters for building successful, sustainable, high-performance organizations.

In recent years Richard has also taken his wealth of knowledge on personal and organization transformation into a new arena: the arena of community and societal transformation. He has used his model and his knowledge of values to develop a global consciousness indicator for nations. When I asked him why such an indicator is important, he replied: "Whatever you can measure, you can manage. The global consciousness indicator for nations allows us to make the evolution of human consciousness, conscious."

Dear reader, I agreed to write this foreword because I truly believe Richard's work provides us with a roadmap for human evolution—a way of building a better world for everyone.

Björn Larsson, CEO, the ForeSight Group
Co-Author: The Rise of The Meaningful Economy

Preface

THIS BOOK SUMMARIZES MY JOURNEY into understanding the importance of values in human decision-making. The journey began around 1990 when I realized I was bored with my career as a transportation engineer. I was 45 years old and had never been bored with my life before, so this was a new experience. I had effectively reached the top of my profession: I was a full-time employee of the World Bank, advising Governments on how to improve their urban transport systems. I lived in a world of economists, planners and engineers. My responsibility was to make sure that the projects being proposed by the Governments were "bankable"—that they met all the criteria necessary for World Bank funding.

As my boredom morphed into depression, I just knew I had to do something different: But what? As I reflected on my life, I realized that my true passion was "transformation" not "transportation." For decades, in my spare time, I had been devouring every book I could find on psychology, spirituality, esoteric philosophy, eastern mysticism and Buddhism. I was fascinated by the topics of transformation and consciousness. The guidance I got, when I meditated on my dilemma, was to write a book. The title came to me immediately, *A Guide to Liberating Your Soul*.[1]

After two years, the book was well advanced, and I started to do public workshops on the topic of Liberating Your Soul. I was still working at the World Bank, but I had changed jobs in 1992 to become Assistant to the Vice President for Environmentally Sustainable Development. Around the same time, I created the World Bank Spiritual Unfoldment Society—a Wednesday lunchtime group devoted to discussing spirituality,

---

[1] Richard Barrett, *A Guide to Liberating Your Soul* (Fulfilling Books: Alexandria), 1995. This book is out of print and has been superseded by *What My Soul Told Me: A Practical Guide to Soul Activation* (Fulfilling Books: Bath), 2012.

consciousness and esoteric philosophy. Around 1994, as I was finishing *A Guide to Liberating Your Soul*, I received guidance on the title for my next book—*Liberating the Corporate Soul*. I started work on it immediately.

In my first book, I developed a model of consciousness based on Vedic philosophy. In my second book, I merged this model with Abraham Maslow's Hierarchy of Needs and built what became known as the Seven Levels of Consciousness model.

I realized, as I was working on *Liberating the Corporate Soul*, that each of the Seven Levels of Consciousness could be defined by specific values. For example, values such as health, wealth and financial stability belonged to the survival level, and friendship, loyalty and caring belonged to the relationship level, and so on. What this meant was that if I knew a person's values, I could determine what levels of consciousness they were operating from, and vice versa; if I knew what levels of consciousness a person was operating from, I would know which values would be important to them. My next step was to extend this idea into organizations—if I could determine an organization's operating values, I would know what levels of consciousness the organization was operating from. The assessment instruments I developed to do this work—to map values to levels of consciousness—became known as the Cultural Transformation Tools.

Around the same time I started working on *Liberating the Corporate Soul*, my Vice President agreed to transfer me to the Organizational Development Department of the World Bank to head up a project on values. For the next two years, I lived and breathed values; at the World Bank, with the project on values, and at home with writing the book *Liberating the Corporate Soul*. By this time, I was fully convinced of the importance of values in decision-making, both in our personal lives and our business lives.

At the same time as my secondment to the Organizational Development Department came to an end—around the middle of 1997—my book, *Liberating the Corporate Soul*, was published by Butterworth-Heinemann.[2] This book, together with the Cultural Transformation Tools, became my passport out of the World Bank. In June 1997, exactly 20 years ago (at the

---

[2] Richard Barrett, *Liberating the Corporate Soul: Building a Visionary Organization* (Butterworth-Heinemann: London) 1998.

time of writing this Preface) I left the World Bank and started a company which later became known as the Barrett Values Centre (BVC).[3]

Since that time, I have never looked back. The most amazing thing is that the Seven Levels of Consciousness model, which I created standing on the shoulders of Vedic philosophy and Abraham Maslow, has never stopped teaching me about consciousness and values. Just what it taught me, is the topic of this book.

I also have to report that I have never stopped getting guidance on what books to write. You will find a list of the books I have written in the front of this book together with the year of publication. Many of these books are available in several languages. To find out more, please go to my website.[4]

---

[3] www.valuescentre.com
[4] www.richardbarrett.net

1

INTRODUCTION

I THINK IT IS VITALLY important at the beginning of a book, especially a book about values, to define the terminology used in the book. To this end, I want to begin by answering the following questions:

- What are values?
- Who are we collectively?
- What is values-based decision-making?
- Are there different types of values?
- What is the purpose of positive ego values?
- What are virtues?
- What are moral values?
- What is ethics?
- What does it mean to live consciously?
- What is a conscience?
- What is the link between values-based decision-making and integrity?

What are values?

I used to refer to values *as a shorthand way of defining whatever is important to you*. Thus, for example, the terms "integrity," "trust," "honesty" and "creativity" could all be regarded as values. The Oxford Dictionary has a similar approach; it defines values as: "one's judgment of what is important in life."

Having worked with and studied values for more than 25 years, I have realized that values are much more than *"what is important"*; they are *the energetic drivers of our aspirations and intentions.* They are the source of all human motivations and decision-making.

If you want to feel the energy behind your values, do the following. Invite a partner or a friend to choose three values that are important to them. Then, choose three values that are important to you. Talk to each other about your respective values, explaining why you believe each value is important. You will notice, as you are doing this exercise, an increase in the conversational energy, and when you have finished, you will notice a feeling of closeness to the person you have been talking to. You will also notice that you share some of the same values.

The reason your energy increases when you talk about your most important values is that your values define who you are at the deepest level of your being. When you talk about your values, you are exposing your soul to the people who are listening. Consequently, being involved in a conversation with another person about your respective values is one of most intimate conversations you can have.

If you want to improve your relationship with someone—your spouse, your children, your business partner, your staff—have a conversation about values. One of the best ways to start such a conversation is to carry out a Personal Values Assessment. You can do this by going to www.valuescentre.com/pva and completing the short survey. A few minutes after completing the survey you will receive a report listing your top ten values by level of consciousness. You can then share your results with the other person, and they can share their results with you.

Most people are not aware of their values. This is because they have never reflected on what is important to them. Taking the time to do a Personal Values Assessment allows you to discover who you are and what motivates you.

Who are we collectively?

At the time of writing, more than 500,000 people had completed a Personal Values Assessment. The top ten values of these people are shown in Figure 1.1 along with the number of people who chose each value. Because of the large number of people who have completed this survey, I tend to think of these values as the values of humanity.

Figure 1.1 is a visual representation of the Seven Levels of Consciousness model. Each shaded dot represents one of the values listed alongside the diagram. The level of consciousness is indicated in brackets, for example, family, caring, respect, and friendship are found at the level 2 relationship level. It is interesting to note that these values are given a higher priority (they got more votes except for humour/fun) than the values at levels 4 and 5 and that the highest scoring value at level 2 is family. You may find it interesting, when you have completed the Personal Values Assessment, to compare your results to the top ten average of these 500,000 people.

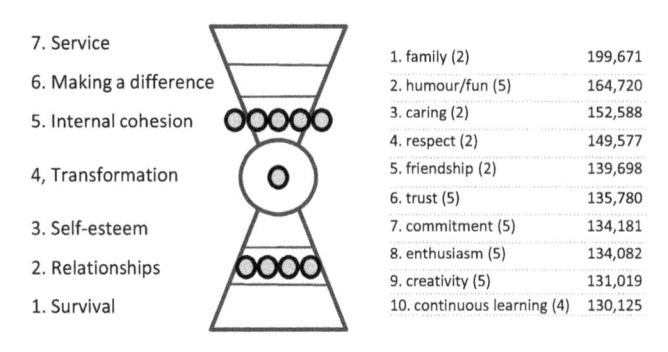

Level		Value	Votes
7. Service		1. family (2)	199,671
6. Making a difference		2. humour/fun (5)	164,720
5. Internal cohesion		3. caring (2)	152,588
		4. respect (2)	149,577
4. Transformation		5. friendship (2)	139,698
		6. trust (5)	135,780
3. Self-esteem		7. commitment (5)	134,181
2. Relationships		8. enthusiasm (5)	134,082
		9. creativity (5)	131,019
1. Survival		10. continuous learning (4)	130,125

Figure 1.1: Top ten values of 500,000 people

After downloading the data for the 500,000 people, we fed the top ten values back into the Personal Values Assessment as if they were a single individual, and this is the report we got.

From the values you selected it is clear that you are a person for whom meaning is important. You have a strong set of moral standards which are important in how you treat others and how you wish to be treated.

Your values show:

- *Having meaningful close relationships with others is important in your life and is central in the decisions you make.*
- *Living with a passionate and an upbeat, fun-loving approach is important to you.*
- *Relationships are a central focus in your life, and you show concern and consideration for those around you.*
- *You demonstrate dedication in all that you do.*

- *Seeking new opportunities to develop and grow keeps you constantly challenged.*
- *You can think imaginatively and use your skills to produce new ideas.*
- *Building confidence in others and wanting others to feel they can rely on you are key factors in your interactions.*

The type of values you selected indicates that the connections you build with others and your individual capabilities are equally important to you.

I believe this value profile tells an interesting story about humanity in general. Five of the top values are about how we relate to the people in our lives—family, caring, respect, friendship, and trust. This suggests that inter-personal safety is a fundamental priority for most people. Historically, personal safety has always been linked to belonging and identity.

Five of the top values are about how we relate to ourselves (who we are)—humour/fun, enthusiasm, commitment, creativity, and continuous learning. This suggests that self-expression is also a fundamental priority. However, the results indicate that we prioritize inter-personal safety over self-expression. Only when we feel safe, do we feel free to express who we are.

This suggests that Maslow's theory is correct. We prioritize safety—a deficiency need over self-actualization—a growth need. Furthermore the ability to develop and grow through continuous learning is of significant importance to us.

The conclusion I reach from this data is we cannot grow and develop unless we feel safe. Once we feel safe, then self-realization becomes our main priority. If we want to build a positive future for everyone, we must create the conditions that allow people to feel safe, especially our children, and support everyone in their self-expression. Feeling safe is intimately linked to belonging and belonging is intimately linked to identity.

What is values-based decision-making?

There are two basic forms of decision-making: belief-based decision-making and values-based decision-making. We either make decisions that align with our beliefs, or we make decisions that align with our values. We begin our lives using our beliefs to make decisions; as we grow older, we shift to using our values to make decisions.

Beliefs are assumptions we hold to be true. They may or may not be true, but we assume they are true.

Most of the beliefs we use for making decisions are formed from our life experiences—especially the experiences we had during the first 24 years of our lives—and from what we were told by our parents and teachers. The most important beliefs we learn during this period of our life are how to survive, keep safe and feel secure in the cultural and environmental framework of our existence. These are the beliefs we learned while our mind-brains are growing and developing—while we are young and impressionable.

The shift from belief-based decision-making to values-based decision-making begins when we reach the individuating stage of development—when we have been able to satisfy our survival, safety and security needs (what Abraham Maslow referred to as deficiency needs) and have the freedom to explore who we are outside our parental programming and cultural conditioning.

Before the twentieth century, very few people individuated: they spent their whole lives living in the same locality—they never traveled very far, and never received a higher education. They never had the possibility to explore other cultures or other ways of being. The only people for whom individuation was an option in earlier times were the educated elites.

Most people today still don't have the possibility of individuating because they either live in poverty—they are preoccupied with trying to meet their deficiency needs—or, they live in a repressive regime or culture which does not tolerate free thinking or self-expression. In such regimes and cultures, fitting in and aligning with the beliefs of the community or nation is the only way to survive, keep safe and feel secure.

With the adoption of democratic governance systems in the 20th century (with free education, improved health care, no travel restrictions and the possibility of prosperity), more and more people were able to meet their survival, safety and security needs, and consequently, could, if they chose to, embrace the individuating stage of development. The resulting shift in consciousness which spawned the self-help movement of the 1960s was instrumental in the lifting of the Iron Curtain in 1991 and was at the root of the Arab Spring in the Middle East and North Africa in 2010.

In all of these cases, increasing levels of education and prosperity enabled a significant number of twenty- and thirty-year-olds to meet their deficiency needs, thereby opening a doorway for them to embrace the individuating stage of development. They were looking for freedom and autonomy: freedom to explore who they were outside their cultural conditioning—the freedom not only to be themselves but also to discover who they were.

Whenever people reach a level of prosperity that allows them to meet their deficiency needs, they automatically seek to have more freedom and autonomy in their lives. They want to live in democratic regimes that embrace the values of equality, accountability, fairness, openness, transparency and trust.

Are there different types of values?

There are two basic types of values—positive values and potentially limiting values. Positive values include terms such as openness, friendship and honesty. Potentially limiting values include terms such as blame, caution and manipulation. The reason I call these negative terms values is because if they weren't valuable to some aspect of our psyche, we would not let them drive our behaviours.

The main difference between positive and potentially limiting values is that positive values come from a place of caring for self or caring for others, whereas potentially limiting values come from the ego's fears about not being able to get its survival, safety or security needs met. In other words, potentially limiting values are self-serving. They make my needs a priority over your needs.

I call them *potentially* limiting values because in some situations they can be more limiting than in others: it depends on the level of fear behind the value and the situation in which the value is expressed. For example, in organizations, bureaucracy is a potentially limiting value. A high level of bureaucracy can be counterproductive in trying to improve performance, whereas a low level of bureaucracy can bring order and efficiency to a chaotic organization thereby improving performance. This is why I regard bureaucracy as a *potentially* limiting value. Some values, such as "blame," for example, are nearly always limiting. They help us to avoid punishment.

Potentially limiting values usually serve our short-term needs. In the long-term, however, potentially limiting values will always be counterproductive. Why? Because potentially limiting values are divisive: they create separation by setting people against each other. For example, it is unlikely that those you have blamed in the past for your wrong-doings will come to your aid in the future.

Other types of values

In addition to positive and limiting values, we can categorize values in other ways. For example, there are values that focus on the needs of an individual (creativity and imagination); values that focus on the needs of relationships (friendship and openness), values that focus on the needs of an organization (profitability and teamwork) and values that focus on the needs of a community or society (internal cohesion and environmental awareness).

Individual values primarily relate to caring about your own needs. For example, freedom, autonomy and creativity are positive individual values, whereas conceit, arrogance and greed are potentially limiting individual values. There is nothing wrong with caring for your own needs; it is only when you put your needs ahead of other people's needs that your values become potentially limiting.

Relationship values are focused on how you interact with other people, be they your friends, family, colleagues or members of your community. For example, caring, trust and fairness are positive relationship values, whereas blame, jealousy and hatred are potentially limiting relationship values.

Organizational values primarily focus on the needs of an organization. For example, profit, teamwork and customer satisfaction are positive organizational values, whereas short-term focus, internal competition and silo mentality are potentially limiting organizational values.

Societal values primarily focus on the needs of a community. For example, environmental awareness, the rule of law and caring for the disadvantaged are positive societal values, whereas violence, discrimination and corruption are potentially limiting societal values.

Another way of categorizing values is to differentiate between values that tend to be embraced by men and values that tend to be embraced by women.

Because of their upbringing men tend to embrace "yang" values, whereas women tend to embrace "yin" values. This is not true for every male and female. Sometimes the situation is reversed. Yang values tend to differentiate people: They include values such as strength, competition and logic—individual values. Yin values tend to connect people: They include values such as compassion, empathy and caring—relationship values.

What is the purpose of positive ego values?

The primary role of the ego is to help us to establish ourselves in the cultural and physical framework of our existence—to support us in surviving, keeping safe and feeling secure. The soul needs the ego to take care of the practicalities of our physical life. Only when we have mastered surviving, keeping safe and feeling secure do we feel we have the freedom to explore our soul nature and our soul's values.

What are virtues?

Virtues are values that are held in high regard by a specific culture, religion or spiritual philosophy. They are held in high regard because they are considered to create harmony among people who share a particular worldview. Virtues are therefore context dependent. There are four classic cardinal virtues—temperance, prudence, courage and justice, and there are three Christian virtues—faith, hope and charity.

In Medieval times there were seven virtues—humility, kindness, temperance, chastity, patience, charity and diligence. In Buddhism there are ten virtuous actions—not to take life, not to take what is not given, avoid sexual misconduct, not to deceive, avoid slander of others, avoid harsh words, avoid empty speech, avoid greedy thoughts, not to be malicious and avoid the wrong view.[5]

---

[5] http://www.rinpoche.com/teachings/conduct.pdf

What are moral values?

Moral values apply to individuals. Like virtues, they are context dependent. They are used to differentiate right action (correct behaviour) from wrong action (incorrect behaviour) within a particular culture (or religion). What is judged as the right action in one culture may be judged as the wrong action in another culture. Consequently, there is no agreement on a universal set of moral values. Moral values usually form part of a code of conduct which sets out the social mores (conventions) and responsibilities of an individual who is part of a particular culture.

What is ethics?

Ethics is a branch of moral philosophy that involves systemizing and recommending concepts of right and wrong conduct. A code of ethics seeks to resolve moral issues—questions of right (acceptable) and wrong (unacceptable) behaviour—within a particular community or professional context. Anyone operating within that context, who fails to abide by the prescribed code of ethics will receive some form of punishment which might include expulsion from the group.

What does it mean to live consciously?

Living consciously means a) being aware of the impact of your actions on others or your environment, and b) seeking to minimize the harm your actions may cause. Living unconsciously means being unaware of the impact of your actions on others or your environment and thereby inadvertently causing harm. When you start to live consciously, you open yourself up to the values, influence and promptings of your soul.

What is a conscience?

Your conscience is an inner guidance system that lets you know when you are *not* living in alignment with your beliefs or values. When you take actions that are not in alignment with your values, you feel guilty. In other words, guilt is a signal you send to yourself when you know you are out of alignment with your deeply held values. When you experience guilt, you also experience remorse—remorse for the wrong you may have caused. Guilt causes you to want to make amends. Therefore the pain of guilt can be a constructive teacher—the experience of guilt can cause us to modify our behaviours—to live more consciously.

What is the link between values-based decision-making and integrity?

Values-based decision-making is the pathway to integrity. Integrity is a state of being and interacting, which is symbolized by the values of honesty, uprightness, decency, wholeness, coherence and cohesion—living in alignment with your soul nature.

People who operate with integrity live by their highest ideals (values). They walk their talk. There is no discrepancy between what they say and how they act. They can be trusted to do the right thing in all circumstances. Their egos and their souls are in alignment. Living in integrity is the pathway to well-being and the pathway to success.

Authenticity is often confused with integrity: they are not the same. Integrity is about the steadfast adherence to a moral or ethical code, for example, the soul's values; whereas authenticity is more about being genuine—true to your origins and sincere in your intentions. There is nothing false, phony or fake about people who operate with authenticity. They are who they are, and they do not pretend to be anything else—they do not mask their true nature. Authenticity and integrity come together—unite—when you live in soul consciousness.

2

Everything I have Learned About Values in My Personal Life

THE SIX MOST IMPORTANT THINGS I have learned about values in my personal life are:

- Our values are a reflection of our needs.
- People get angry when their needs are not met.
- Our value priorities change as we move through the seasons of our lives.
- Our value priorities change depending on our life circumstances.
- At the deepest level of our being, we all share the same universal values.
- Values unite and beliefs separate.

Our values are a reflection of our needs

Whatever we need—whatever is important to us—is what we value. Conversely, if we don't need something—if something is not important to us—we don't value it. This is just as true for our possessions as it is for the people in our lives. You can tell what people value in their lives—what they need—by what they pay attention to, by what and who they care about, and how and on what they spend their time.

Here, for example, are my top ten values. These are the things I value; the things I care about; the important things I need in my life. The grey dots on this diagram show my values mapped to the Seven Levels of Consciousness model. The number in brackets after the value indicates the level of consciousness to which the value belongs.

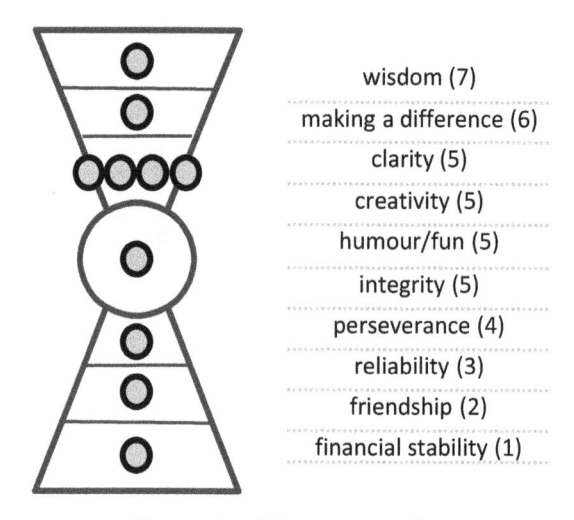

wisdom (7)
making a difference (6)
clarity (5)
creativity (5)
humour/fun (5)
integrity (5)
perseverance (4)
reliability (3)
friendship (2)
financial stability (1)

Figure 2.1: My top ten values

What you notice in this diagram is that my top ten values are spread over the Seven Levels of Consciousness. This means, generally speaking, that I can handle all the challenges that life throws at me. I would hope, having reached the ripe old age of 72, that this is true. I've had plenty of time to practice. I know I still trip up, but less than I used to. When your top ten values are spread over all levels of consciousness, you are said to be operating from Full-Spectrum Consciousness.

This is what BVC's Personal Values Assessment says about my values:

Your values indicate that you are able to lead a balanced and fulfilled life. From the values you selected it is clear that you are a person for whom meaning is important. You have a strong set of moral standards which are important in how you treat others and how you wish to be treated.

Your values show:

- *You have a gift for thinking imaginatively and using your skills to help you make positive changes in the lives of others.*
- *You like to ensure information is clearly understood and expressed.*

- *Remaining in control of your finances and ensuring that you are not over-stretched provides you with comfort.*
- *Having meaningful close relationships with others is important in your life.*
- *You have a fun-loving approach to life and enjoy sharing good times.*
- *You are true to yourself and your principles and try to live your life accordingly.*
- *Demonstrating determination and resolution to follow through, ensures you can fulfill your aims.*
- *You are dependable and you want others to know that they can count on you.*
- *Experience has provided you with insight and understanding, enabling you to think clearly and guide others.*

The type of values you selected indicates that your individual capabilities are most important to you. From your choice of values, you also demonstrate care for the greater good.

What does BVC's Personal Values Assessment say about you? Check it out at www.valuescentre.com/pva.

Towards the end of the report you receive, you will find a series of exercises. The first exercise asks you to choose your top three values and explore why these are important to you. This will help you to understand how your values influence your actions and why you may respond with irritation or anger if someone violates one of your values.

The second exercise asks you to think about the values you would like to demonstrate more fully in your life. Completing these two exercises will help you to build an action plan to support your self-development.

It is worth reviewing your values frequently to see if there have been any changes. As we move through the seasons of our life, our value priorities change from being more focused on self-interest to being more focused on the common good.

People get angry when their needs are not met

Almost every hour of every day, every person on the planet is focused on the same thing: getting their needs met. There is hardly any activity we undertake that does not involve us in some way trying to satisfy our needs—keeping fit, relaxing to music, singing in a choir, raising kids, etc.; they are all attempts to satisfy a need. Even when we are helping others to get their needs met, we are usually attempting to satisfy our own need to make a difference or be of service.

Not surprisingly, therefore, our emotions are linked to the satisfaction or non-satisfaction of our needs. We experience anger when our needs are not met. We experience happiness when we can satisfy a need that previously had not been met. We experience anxiety when we believe our needs will not be met in the future, and we experience contentment when we feel all our needs are being met.

What about the emotions of joy and sadness? I believe these are the emotions of the soul. Unlike the ego which has needs, the soul has desires. When the desires of the soul are met, we feel joy. When the desires of the soul are not met, we experience sadness. Repeated experiences of sadness lead to depression.[6]

Because needs and values are intimately entwined, you must also recognize that when you see your most important values being violated, you can get angry. For example, when you regard fairness as one of your most important values, you will get angry if you encounter situations where you feel you are being treated unfairly or you see others being treated unfairly.

Because our needs are so important to us, I think it is important to understand what a need is. I define a need as:

A real or imagined lack of something that is essential for maintaining the body's physiological (biological) stability or the ego's emotional stability.

You know you have an unmet ego need whenever you experience anxiety, anger, frustration, impatience or any other form of emotional instability. Behind every form of emotional instability you will always find fear. The emotion of fear and its derivatives are signs that you either have a belief that something is lacking, or a belief that something you have that is important to the satisfaction of your needs, may be taken away.

---

[6] Richard Barrett, *A New Psychology of Human Well-Being: The Influence of Ego-Soul Dynamics on Mental and Physical Health* (Fulfilling Books: London), 2016.

What you are saying, when you believe you have an ego need is: My life conditions are not perfect because I lack something that is necessary for my body to go on functioning (physical survival), or for my mind to feel that I am loved and protected (safe among people), and respected and recognized (secure in my community).

When you understand that nothing is lacking from your life—when you consider your life is perfect the way it is; when you are grateful for what you have and consider what you have to be sufficient—then will you begin to feel a sense of contentment: you will be living in soul consciousness.

This understanding, that anger arises from an unmet need, is crucial to understanding how to overcome disharmony and connect with people. Whenever you are in front of someone who is angry, frustrated or impatient, recognize that their upset is a sign of an unmet need. They may not be aware of their unmet need, so asking, "What need do you have at this moment that is not being met?", may help to diffuse the situation or at least bring clarity to what the upset is about.

Our value priorities change as we move through the seasons of our lives

As we get older, our value priorities change. What we valued as a baby is not what we value as a teenager; what we valued as a teenager is not what we value as a mature adult or as someone in their retirement years.

Despite the changing nature of our value priorities, there are three things that we value at all ages—survival, safety and security. These three needs are so important to us that they are hardwired into our brains. When they are not satisfied, they dominate our conscious and subconscious thinking. We become anxious and fearful if we think our survival, safety or security needs are not being met in the present, and may not be met in the future. However, when these needs are met, we give them no further thought.

We can define the seasons of our lives as seven stages—I call these the seven stages of psychological development. Each stage has its own needs, and therefore its own values.

The first three stages are linked to the physical development of our brain and the emotional and mental development of our mind. Every repeated experience during the first twenty-four years of our lives lays down new synaptic connections in the brain. We call these synaptic connections beliefs. By the time we reach our mid-twenties the reptilian mind-brain has developed a set of unconscious beliefs about surviving, the limbic mind-brain has developed a set of subconscious beliefs about keeping safe, and our neo-cortex mind-brain has developed a set of conscious beliefs about feeling secure.

Surviving

For the first three months of life, from the moment of conception to the formation of the reptilian mind-brain, the soul-mind is the dominant (conscious) interface with the embryo's external world—the mother's womb. The species-mind, which is subconscious of the soul-mind, guides the development of the embryo into a fetus and creates a functioning body-mind (reptilian mind-brain) by around the third trimester of gestation.

When the body-mind becomes operational, it becomes the new conscious interface with the external world, and the soul-mind becomes the subconscious of the body-mind. The species-mind (encapsulated in the coding of DNA) then becomes the unconscious of the body-mind, guiding the development of the body through to maturity.

The primary focus of the body-mind is staying alive. It does this by regulating the body's internal stability. Because of our species programming (DNA), the body-mind instinctively knows how to manage the body's homeostatic functioning, and once the baby is born, it knows how to suckle and cry (for help) if it feels discomforting sensations.

From the moment of conception, the embryo, the fetus and the baby are completely dependent on the mother for their sense of well-being. The experiences that the fetus and baby have while the body-mind is learning to be in our three-dimensional material reality (forming memories) lead to the formation of the young child's subconscious beliefs—the body-mind's autobiographical memory imprints (beliefs) that it uses to make-meaning.

Although the body-mind knows how to react to any internal stability, such as hunger, thirst, being too hot or being too cold, it doesn't know how to alleviate these sensations. If the baby's reactions (grimacing, crying, etc.) to these discomforting sensations result in getting its needs met, it feels loved. If its reactions go unnoticed or are ignored, it becomes increasingly distressed—it feels fear.

Gradually the baby begins to link its reaction to its sensations and the response it gets. It realizes that through its reactions it is able, or as the case may be, not able, to control its sense of well-being. If its needs are "magically" met, it feels in control of its world. If its needs are not met, it does not feel in control of its world.

The problem the fetus and the new-born baby have is that they still believe they are living in an energetic field of connectedness and love. They are living in soul consciousness because they have not yet learned about separation. The baby gradually learns through the experience of uncomfortable sensations that it is no longer living in that world.

At this point, usually around 18 months to 2 years, the "pain" (lack of love) of experiencing discomfort and the feeling of separation becomes too much for the soul to bear. It filters out this pain by creating the psychic entity we call the ego to act as a buffer from the world of uncomfortable sensations; from pain, fear and separation.

If the mother or caregivers of the baby are not vigilant, or if the baby is abused, left alone or abandoned for long periods of time, the baby will form subconscious beliefs that the world it lives in is an unsafe place and that it is not loved. After that, throughout his or her life, this person will seek to control what is happening in their environment to make sure they get their needs get met. Such a person will be cautious and vigilant and tend to micro-manage whatever is going on around them that might affect their well-being.

If on the other hand, the mother or caregivers of the baby are attentive to its needs and are watchful and responsive to signs of distress, then the baby will grow up with the feeling of being loved and that the world it lives in is a safe place. The feeling of control and competence the baby gets when its needs are quickly met is an essential prerequisite for mastering the self-actualization stage of development later in life. If you don't feel in control and competent, you will not be prepared to take the risks that the journey into self-actualization may entail.

At the survival stage of development, love is experienced through the satisfaction of our physiological needs. This is when the body-mind experiences stability. The body-mind experiences instability—a lack of love—when it feels abandoned and uncared for.

Conforming

Towards the end of the surviving stage of development, the infant becomes mobile and learns to communicate. This is the time when the ego begins to form and the limbic mind-brain (emotional mind), which has been developing in the background, becomes the dominant mind-brain. The focus of the emotional mind is always on safety and protection—keeping safe from harm—by finding a "home" where we feel cared for and protected. The body-mind goes on functioning in the background as the physical interface with the world, and the emotional mind becomes the social interface with the world.

When the emotional mind becomes dominant, the body-mind becomes the subconscious of the emotional mind and the soul-mind is pushed further into the background. It becomes the unconscious of the emotional mind. It is still able to influence the thoughts of the child but less directly than before.

While the emotional mind is dominant, it uses the memories stored in the body-mind and soul-mind for meaning-making and decision-making. Some of the impulses and reactions of the body-mind can be overridden by the emotional mind if the emotional mind believes these reactions could compromise its ability to get its future safety needs met.

If for example, the child feels unfairly treated, instead of becoming angry and blaming its parents, the child may turn the anger it is feeling about not getting its needs met inwards, blaming itself for its feelings of discomfort and emotional instability. The child blames itself because it is afraid to show anger towards its parents. If it did show anger towards its parents, it might be more difficult to get its safety needs met in the future. This emotional instability does not go away. It is always there in the background influencing our subconscious decision-making. This is the beginning of the development of the critical voice in our heads; the voice of judgment about not being worthy enough to receive the love we are seeking. We blame ourselves, rather than blaming our parents for not getting our needs met.

If the parents make the child's adherence to rules conditional on the child getting its desires met, or if the child is coerced into behaving in specific ways, the child will learn that love is conditional, and will try to use that strategy later in life to get its needs met.

At the beginning of this stage of development, the child may resort to temper tantrums to get its needs met. The young infant has not yet learned how to separate itself from its needs. Neither has it learned that the people it depends on for its survival and safety also have needs.

If the parents give in to the child's temper tantrums, the child quickly learns that behaving "badly" is a good strategy for getting its needs met. When this happens, the parent's lives become intolerable—they become totally ruled by their children.

For the sake of family unity, the growth of the child's ego has to be managed. There are two ways of doing this: the correct way—by gradual socialization (getting the child to recognize that other people may also have needs); and the incorrect way—by attempting to crush the ego through force or punishment.

If the parents are firm but loving, the child will learn to follow the rules the parents have laid down. It learns that life is more pleasant and enjoyable, less threatening and less difficult, if it can live in a state of harmony with its caregivers and siblings. The child learns that conforming—obeying the rules—has benefits. It allows the child to get its physical and emotional needs met *and* feel loved. It also learns that obeying the rules avoids the pain of punishment and the feeling of separation.

If the child's parents or caregivers are attentive to the child's needs, if it is raised in a caring, loving environment where it feels safe and protected, then the child will grow up with the desire and willingness to form committed relationships and conform to society's rules when it reaches adulthood. Participating in family rituals is important at this stage of development because they contribute to the child's feelings of belonging and safety.

Learning to feel safe, comfortable and loved at the conforming stage of development is an essential prerequisite for mastering the integrating stage of development later in life. If you don't feel safe with others—if you don't trust them—you will find it difficult to cooperate with others when you become an adult.

At the conforming stage of development, love is experienced through the satisfaction of our safety and protection needs. This is when the emotional mind experiences stability. The emotional mind experiences instability—a lack of love—when its love and belonging needs are not met.

Differentiating

Towards the end of the conforming stages of development, around the age of 7 or 8, the neocortex mind-brain (rational mind) which has been developing in the background, becomes dominant. The focus of the rational mind is primarily on security—keeping us safe from harm and supporting us in finding our place in the world. The rational mind gradually takes over from the emotional mind as our conscious interface with the world. The emotional mind goes on operating in the background as our social interface with the world and the body-mind goes on operating in the background as our "biological" interface with the world.

When the rational mind becomes dominant, the emotional mind becomes the subconscious of the rational mind, and the body-mind becomes the unconscious of the rational mind. The soul-mind becomes the super unconscious. Its influence is felt only faintly, if felt at all.

Subconscious decisions made by the emotional mind can be overridden by the rational mind if the rational mind believes the reactions of the emotional mind would compromise its ability to get our security needs met—this is what is referred to as emotional intelligence.

At this stage of development, as the child becomes a teenager, it is beginning to explore the world outside of its family and home. Whereas parental and sibling relations were of significant importance to the child's safety up to the age of about eight, when the child gets close to its teens its relations with its peers and the authority figures in its life, such as teachers or religious instructors, becomes important for its security needs. The teenager gets its security needs met, by finding ways to associate with (belong to) a community, group, or a gang or by staying close to its parents. To get its security needs met the teenager must find a way to become respected and recognized by the members of the group it wants to associate with or by its parents.

There are three avenues open to a teenager to get its respect and recognition needs met:

- By displays of force and strength—becoming strong or powerful (for girls, by becoming beautiful). This is usually the route taken to get our recognition needs met from a gang.

- By displays of knowledge and learning—becoming a good student. This is usually the route taken to get our recognition needs met from our parents.
- By displays of "coolness" (status)—having the latest technologies, hair style, etc. This is usually the route taken to get our recognition needs met from our peers.

The path the teenager chooses will depend to a large extent on a) his or her natural physical endowments, b) the social environment in which he or she lives, and c) the relationship he or she has with his or her parents and siblings. The most important of these is the relationship the teenager has with his or her parents.

If the teenager is respected and recognized by its parents—the parents spend time with the teenager, provide emotional support to the teenager, and help them take up studies that interest the teenager—or that align with their natural talents—the teenager will not be dependent on seeking respect and recognition from his or her peers, a gang or other authority figures in the teenager's life.

If the teenager joins a gang, taking on dares can become a rite of passage for membership. This may lead young people "off the straight and narrow." They may do things they know to be wrong simply to belong to a group where they can feel recognized and feel secure. Teenagers who form relationships with an adult outside of the home to get their recognition needs met leave themselves open to religious radicalization or sexual grooming.

What is important at this stage of development is for teenagers to get positive feedback from their parents. If they do not get positive feedback, they will seek to get it from other people. They will join a group or gang where they feel accepted and valued; where they feel accepted for who they are, and their gifts, skills or talents are recognized.

This may create conflict in their life at home because they may get caught between two value systems: the value system of their parents, and the value system of the group or gang to which they belong. If this situation is not handled sensitively by their parents, home life will become difficult and may become intolerable. The teenager may rebel.

From a parental perspective, guiding rather than controlling, allowing rather than preventing, encouraging rather than denigrating and trusting rather than doubting, gives teenagers space to safely explore who they are and find their sense of identity in the larger world outside the family home.

Feeling physically and emotionally secure in your community—having a healthy sense of self-esteem by being respected and recognized by others—is an essential prerequisite for mastering the serving stage of development later in life. If you don't feel secure in your community during your teenage years, you will not feel confident in making a contribution to society later in life.

At the differentiating stage of development, love is experienced through the satisfaction of our security needs. This is when the rational mind experiences stability. The rational mind experiences instability—a lack of love—when its respect and recognition needs are not met.

Individuating

Around your mid-twenties, you begin to feel the soul's impulse to connect with your soul-self. For this to happen, you will need to break the chains of dependency that keep you tied to the parental and cultural framework of your existence. You are finished with being dependent on others for the satisfaction of your needs; you are seeking independence. You will want to find freedom and autonomy, and you will want to become responsible and accountable for every aspect of your life, in particular, you will want to embrace and express your values.

Thus, the task at the individuating stage of development is to embark on the journey that leads to the recovery of your soul. Without fully realizing it, you will be dis-embedding yourself from your parental and cultural background and begin to align the motivations of your ego with the motivations of your soul.

For those who were fortunate enough to have been brought up by self-actualized parents, to have lived in a community or culture where freedom and independence are celebrated, where higher education was easily available, where men and women are treated equally, and where you are encouraged from a young age to express your needs and think for yourself, you will find it relatively easy to move through the individuating stage of psychological development, that is, as long as you can find work that enables you to make a living. If you cannot find work that gives you financial independence, you will feel demoralized because you will not have the freedom you need to individuate.

Many find it difficult to extract themselves from the influence of their parents. Others, such as those who live in authoritarian communities or repressive regimes, may be afraid to express themselves because they don't want to be punished for breaking the rules or don't want to be locked up for speaking their truth. Thus, if you were brought up by controlling parents, if you live in an authoritarian regime or if you are discriminated against because of your gender, sexual preferences, religion or race, and you developed fears about being able to meet your deficiency needs, you are likely to have difficulties moving through the individuating stage of development. Your fears will keep you anchored in the lower levels of consciousness.

Thus, your task at this stage of development it to master these fears so you are no longer dependent on others for your self-esteem, for your protection, and your survival. If you do not master these fears they will continue to show up in your life and make it difficult to master the next three stages of development.

You have not yet figured out that you are a soul, and your soul has a purpose for your life. The soul needs you to become viable and fully independent in the framework of your existence because whatever you are dependent on dominates you. If you are dominated by your deficiency needs, your soul will not be able to express itself.

Self-actualizing

If you can successfully master the individuating stage of development, when you reach your forties, sometimes a little earlier and sometimes a little later, you will begin to feel the impulse of your soul to express itself more fully in your life. You will experience the soul's desire for self-expression as the need to find meaning. You will be looking for a vocation or calling that aligns with your soul's purpose. This means uncovering your natural gifts and talents and making them available to the world.

For most people, finding their vocation or calling usually begins with a feeling of unease or boredom about their job, profession or chosen career—with the work they thought would enable them to feel secure by providing them with a good income and prospects for advancement leading to increased wealth, status or power.

Uncovering your soul's purpose not only brings vitality to your life, it also sparks your creativity. You will become more intuitive and spend more time in a state of flow; being present in what you are doing, and feeling committed and passionate about your work.

Mastering the self-actualizing stage of development can be challenging, especially if your vocation or calling offers less security than the job, profession or career you trained for earlier in your life. You may feel scared or uncomfortable embarking in a new direction that does not pay the rent or finance your children's education but does bring meaning and purpose to your life. This is why it so important at this stage of development to master your survival fears. Knowing you can take care of yourself gives you the confidence you need to explore your self-expression. If you are afraid that you might not be able to survive doing what you love to do, you may deny your soul expression. This will lead to suffering and depression.

Some people find their vocation early in their lives, others discover it much later; some spend their whole lives searching. Uncovering and embracing your soul's purpose is vitally important because it is the key to living a fulfilling life.

Integrating

If you were successful in traversing the individuating stage of development and found your soul's purpose at the self-actualizing stage, when you reach your fifties, you will want to use your gifts and talents to make a difference in the world. To do this, you will need to connect with others; to form caring relationships with those you want to help and those you want to collaborate with to leverage your impact in the world. Connecting with others who share your passion or calling and with those who will be the beneficiaries of your gifts and talents is essential for mastering this stage of development.

To connect with and support others, you will need to tap into your emotional intelligence and empathy skills. You will need to feel what others are feeling if you are truly going to help them. Thus, how well you mastered the conforming stage of development will significantly influence your progress through the integrating stage of development.

Knowing you can handle your relationship needs—knowing you are lovable and can love others—gives you the confidence you need to successfully manage this stage of development. In addition, you must also be able to cooperate with others by assuming a larger sense of identity and shift from being independent to being interdependent.

Some people get so wrapped up in themselves at the self-actualizing stage that they are unable to make this shift. They get lost in their creativity, focusing only on their contribution, rather than the larger contribution they could make if they were able to connect with others. Working with others in service to the common good is more likely to bring a sense of fulfillment than working on your own at this stage of your life.

Serving

The last stage of development follows naturally from the integrating stage. I call this the serving stage of development. This stage of development usually begins to occur in your early sixties, sometimes a little earlier, sometimes a little later. The focus of this stage of development is on self-less service to the community you identify with. What you are feeling is the soul's desire for contribution.

How well you mastered the differentiating stage of development will significantly influence your progress through the serving stage of development. Having a healthy sense of self-esteem will give you the confidence to make your gifts and talents available to those who need them.

It does not matter how big or small your contribution is, what is important is fulfilling your soul's purpose. Alleviating suffering, caring for the disadvantaged and building a better society are some of the activities you may want to explore at this stage of your life. On the other hand, your contribution may be simply caring for the life of another soul.

As you enter the serving stage of development, you will find yourself becoming more introspective and reflective—looking for ways to deepen your sense of connection to your soul and beyond your soul to the deeper levels of your being—connecting to whatever you consider divine. You may become a keeper of wisdom, an elder of the community or a person to whom younger people turn for guidance or mentoring.

As you make progress with this stage of development, you will uncover new levels of compassion in your life. You will experience feelings of well-being and fulfillment that you never experienced before. You will begin to see how connected we all are; how, by serving others, you are serving your larger self. At this level of consciousness, giving becomes the same as receiving. To experience these feeling more profoundly, you will want to become the servant of your soul. Eventually, you may realize that you don't have a soul; you are your soul: you are the living the life of an energetic being in material awareness.

Summary

The tasks and needs we must master at each stage of development are shown in Table 2.1

Table 2.1: The tasks and needs associate with the seven stages of psychological development

Stage of development	Age range	Task	Need
Serving	60 + years	Contributing to the well-being of others.	To be of service to humanity.
Integrating	50 – 59 years	Connecting in unconditional loving relationships.	To make a difference in your world.
Self-actualizing	40 – 49 years	Discovering and expressing your gifts and talents.	To find meaning and purpose.
Individuating	25 – 39 years	Finding freedom to discover who you are.	To feel you can operate with autonomy.
Differentiating	8 – 24 years	Feeling accepted, respected and recognized.	To feel a sense of self-worth.
Conforming	2 – 8 years	Feeling safe, protected and loved.	To feel a sense of belonging.
Surviving	0 – 2 years	Feeling physically cared for and nurtured.	To feel in control of your life.

No matter what age you are at, to grow and develop you must address the fears and anxieties you have about being able to meet your deficiency (survival, safety and security) needs. Also, if you are at the individuating stage of development, you must be able to master your fear of leaving those you are dependent on—your parents and the community you were brought up in—to find the freedom to be who you are and operate with autonomy. If you were brought up by self-actualized parents, this would not be so difficult because they will understand.

If you are at the self-actualizing stage of development—finding and engaging in the work you are passionate about—you must be able to master your survival fears; to feel you are in control of your life and not a victim. If you are at the integrating stage of development—connecting with others in unconditional loving relationships to make a difference—you must be able to master you relationship fears; to feel loved enough to feel safe in loving others. If you are at the serving stage of development—contributing to the well-being of society—you must be able to master your self-esteem fears; to feel confident enough to go out into the world and offer your gifts and talents. Table 2.2 shows the concerns and feelings that could prevent you from mastering each stage of development.

Table 2.2: Concerns and feelings associated with the mastery of each stage of development

Stage of development	Concerns	Feelings
Serving	Lack of confidence and isolation	I feel I have nothing to offer my community.
Integrating	Lack of connection and loneliness	I feel I have nothing in common with the people around me.
Self-actualizing	Lack of purpose/meaning in your life	I feel blocked in expressing my gifts and talents.
Individuating	Lack of freedom and autonomy	I feel trapped and can't find a way to be myself.
Differentiating	Lack of recognition in your community	I feel like I do not belong. I feel insecure.

Conforming	Lack of harmony in relationships	I don't feel loved or protected. I feel unsafe.
Surviving	Lack of health or income	I feel vulnerable. I do not have what I need to survive.

We feel a sense of well-being when we can satisfy the needs of the stage of development we are at. We experience flourishing when we have found our meaning and purpose, can connect with others to make a difference and feel confident enough to contribute to the well-being of our community.[7]

Our value priorities change depending on our life circumstances

Just as we can mark where we are in the passage of our lives by the seven stages of development model, we can mark where we are at any moment of the day by the Seven Levels of Consciousness model.

Normally, the level of consciousness we operate from will coincide with the stage of development we have reached. However, if we encounter a situation that triggers one of our limiting survival, safety or security beliefs we will immediately drop down to one of the first three levels of consciousness. For example, if I am 36 years old—in the middle of the individuating stage of development—and I lose my job and my savings, I will immediately drop down to the survival level of consciousness because I will need to find some income to pay for my basic needs.

The seven levels of personal consciousness are shown in Table 2.3. The first column names the stages of psychological development. The second column names the level of consciousness that corresponds to the stage of psychological development. The third column indicates some of the positive values that are found at each level of consciousness, and the fourth column indicates some of the potentially limiting values that show up at the first three levels of consciousness.

---

[7] www.valuescentre.com/flourishing

Table 2.3: The positive and limiting values associated with the seven levels of personal consciousness

Stages of development		Levels of consciousness	Positive values	Potentially limiting values
Serving	7	Service	Compassion, forgiveness, humility, contribution, future generations.	Not applicable
Integrating	6	Making a difference	Collaboration, empathy, intuition, mentoring, partnering, alliances.	Not applicable
Self-actualizing	5	Internal cohesion	Honesty, trust, creativity, integrity, authenticity, meaning, internal alignment.	Not applicable
Individuating	4	Transformation	Freedom, autonomy, accountability, adaptability, courage, personal growth.	Not applicable
Differentiating	3	Self-esteem	Security, recognition, positive self-image, self-esteem, confidence.	Arrogance, pride, conceit, superiority.
Conforming	2	Relationships	Safety, family, friendship, belonging, harmony.	Being liked, jealousy, revenge.

Stages of development	Levels of consciousness	Positive values	Potentially limiting values
Surviving	1 Survival	Survival, health, physical fitness, nutrition, financial stability.	Control, greed, caution.

Here is a brief description of the Seven Levels of Consciousness.

Level 1: Survival consciousness

The first level of personal consciousness is all about survival. To survive, we need clean air, water and wholesome food to keep our bodies healthy and fit, and we need to feel financially secure.

How you deal with survival situations as an adult depends on the conditioning you received as a baby. If you had difficulties getting your survival needs met—your parents ignored you when you cried, or you felt abandoned—you will be very cautious as an adult. Whenever you have anything that feels like a survival challenge, your fear-based limiting beliefs from childhood will be triggered. You may become anxious and emotionally upset. Your anxiety will come from the limiting belief that you will not be able to control your environment to get your needs met. If on the other hand, your needs were always met as a baby, you will be able to handle survival situations without too much stress. In this case, no matter what happens, you will feel confident in being able to control the situation.

Level 2: Relationship consciousness

The second level of personal consciousness is all about safety. To feel safe, we need to feel loved and protected. We need to feel a sense of belonging.

How you deal with relationship situations as an adult depends on the conditioning you received as a child. If you had difficulties getting your safety needs met during the conforming stage of development, you will be suspicious of others as an adult. Whenever you experience anything that feels like a relationship challenge—when you don't feel loved, or feel protected—your fear-based limiting beliefs from childhood will be triggered, and you may become anxious and emotionally upset. If on the other hand, you felt unconditionally loved as a child and always felt safe and protected, you will be able to handle safety situations without too much stress.

Level 3: Self-esteem consciousness

The third level of personal consciousness is about feeling secure in your community. To feel secure, we need to feel accepted and respected by our peers and recognized by those in positions of authority in our community.

How you deal with self-esteem challenges as an adult depends on the conditioning you received as a teenager. If you had difficulties getting your security needs met during the differentiating stage of development, you will lack confidence as an adult. Whenever you experience anything that feels like a self-esteem challenge—when you don't feel good enough—your fear-based limiting beliefs from your teenage years will be triggered, and you may become anxious and emotionally upset. If on the other hand, you were acknowledged and recognized for who you were as a teenager—if you always felt accepted and had a good relationship with your parents, peers and authority figures—you will be able to handle security situations without too much stress.

Level 4: Transformation consciousness

The fourth level of human consciousness is about finding freedom and autonomy, so you discover who you are beyond the parental programming and cultural conditioning of your formative years. At this stage of development, you will find yourself asking "Who am I?" and "What is important to me?" Only when you find answers to these questions, will you discover your true (soul) self.

Fully expressing who you are without fear of what others may think or say, particularly your parents, peers, spouse and the authority figures in your life, gives you the opportunity to make choices that are more in alignment with who you are. The prize that comes with the pursuit of this self-understanding and knowledge is the ability to operate with integrity. When you discover and express who you are, you no longer need to hide behind a façade. You can remove your ego (personality) mask and march to your tune, not to the tune that has been imposed on you by others.

To find out who you are, you will want to embrace adventure, and you will want to discover and hone your skills and talents. If you grew up with self-actualized parents in a liberal democracy, you will already have an advantage. You will have few subconscious limiting fears, and you will feel free to express your true nature—the values you hold deep in your heart.

Level 5: Internal cohesion consciousness

The fifth level of human consciousness is about finding meaning in your life—finding what your soul came into the world to do. At this level of consciousness, the question is no longer "Who am I?" but "Why am I here in this body?" For those who do not feel any sense of purpose, this can be a daunting inquiry. For others, who are gifted with a particular talent, your purpose will be obvious.

If you are not sure of your purpose, simply focus on what you love to do and pay attention to what is immediately in front of you. Whatever it is, do it to the best of your ability. Alternatively just follow your joy, develop your most obvious talents, and pursue your passion.

Many people do not find their purpose until quite late in life. However, when they look back, they realize that all the twists and turns had a reason—to prepare you to give the gift you were born to give—to fully express your true nature.

When you find your purpose, it may feel like something small, or it may feel like something large. Whatever it is, you need to recognize that it is what your soul came to do, and if you follow the promptings of your soul you will find a sense of meaning and fulfillment in your life. Your life will become a journey of synchronicity, constantly unfolding in front of you. Be assured, when you commit your energy to your soul purpose, all manner of unexpected events will occur to support you.

When you fail to express soul-given gifts and talents, you will experience sadness and depression. You won't feel good in your skin. You may feel a sense of hopelessness. You can't explain what is wrong; you will just know you are not fulfilling your potential.

Level 6: Making a difference consciousness

The sixth level of human consciousness is about making a difference in the world—in your family, your workplace, in your community or nation, or in our global society.

If you are a leader operating at this level of consciousness, you will realize that your ability to fulfill your purpose is strongly conditioned by your ability to connect with others and facilitate the work of those who support you. Enlightened leaders understand that it is through others—their followers—that they make an impact in the world. The more easily you can connect and empathize with others, the easier it will be to fulfill your destiny.

The focus of making a difference consciousness is on aligning your energies with your soul purpose. This may mean giving up a way of life that brings you comfort, stability and certainty. It may mean moving location, giving up friends, or risking your financial stability. In short, it may feel scary. But it is not something you should avoid. You will never be at ease with yourself—you will not find internal stability—if you do not follow your passion. If you don't follow the promptings of your soul, you will spend the rest of your life feeling unfulfilled, depressed or living with regrets.

Level 7: Service consciousness

The seventh level of human consciousness is about selfless service to the cause or the work you were born to do. You reach this level of consciousness when making a difference becomes a way of life. You are now fully imbued with your soul's purpose and living the life of a soul-infused personality. You are at ease with uncertainty and embrace whatever opportunities come your way. You feel as if you are being guided by your soul.

When you reach this stage of development, you may find yourself needing time for quiet and reflection. You will be seeking the inspiration you need from your soul so that you can live and breathe your purpose every moment of your life. You will know when you are operating from this level of consciousness because there will be nothing else for you to do. You will not want to "retire" because that would close down your self-expression and take meaning out of your life. What you previously considered work, now becomes your play. At this level of consciousness, you let the doing flow through the being.

Full-Spectrum consciousness

When you reach the latter years of your life, you may be fortunate enough to have learned how to master every stage of psychological development—your ego needs and your soul desires—and you will be able to operate from Full-Spectrum Consciousness. When you are operating from Full-Spectrum Consciousness, you can respond appropriately to all situations that life throws at you with inner calm—without fear, upset or anxiety. Individuals experiencing Full-Spectrum Consciousness display the following attributes:

They master their survival needs by staying healthy, assuring their physiological survival and their financial security and keeping safe from harm and injury.

They master their relationship needs by building friendships and family connections that create a sense of love and belonging.

They master their self-esteem needs by building a strong sense of self-worth and acting responsibly and reliably in everything they do.

They master their transformation needs by having the courage to embrace their authentic selves; living their values and managing or overcoming the fears that keep them focused on their deficiency needs.

They master their internal cohesion needs by uncovering and embracing their soul's purpose, expressing their creativity and thereby finding meaning in life.

They master their making a difference needs through actualizing their sense of purpose and leveraging their actions in the world by collaborating with others in unconditional loving relationships.

They master their service needs by devoting their life to their purpose and leading a life of selfless service for the good of humanity and the planet.

At the deepest level of our being, we all share the same universal values

On the surface, we all look, dress and behave differently. We have different racial characteristics, we observe different religions, we come from different cultures with different traditions, and we have different worldviews.

However, at the deepest level of our being, we are all the same: we all share the same hopes and aspirations because we are all on the same journey and we all share the same values, because we all have the same human needs.

Beneath the veneer of our physical characteristics and our cultural heritage, we are energetic souls participating in a human physical experience. We are attempting to learn the same things: how to survive, keep safe and feel secure—satisfy our ego's needs; how to find freedom and autonomy so we can be who we really are; how to express our unique gifts and talents; how to connect with others in unconditional loving relationships to make a difference; and how to use our gifts and talents to contribute to the well-being of humanity—satisfying our soul's desires.

The difference between the needs of the ego and the desires of the soul is that the former enables us to establish ourselves in the cultural and physical framework of our existence—survive, keep safe and feel secure—and the latter enables us to fully express who we are at the deepest level of our being—access our natural gifts and talents and thereby make a difference through the contribution we can make in society.

The soul has three primary motivations: self-expression, connection and contribution. Self-expression means allowing the creativity of the soul to flow through your being by fully expressing who you are. From the ego's perspective, this means finding meaning and purpose in life. Once you have found meaning and purpose—when you dare to express your innate gifts and talents—the soul wants to make use of your gifts and talents. From the ego's perspective, this means making a difference. To make a difference we need to be able to connect with others in unconditional loving relationships. If you have difficulties connecting, you may have difficulties making a difference. Once you have learned how to connect, all you want to do is to be of service—to contribute to the well-being of humanity and the planet.

Only when we have learned how to express our innate gifts and talents—the things that bring passion and joy to our life—and then learned how to connect with others are we able to fully contribute. Thus we can identify three types of soul values:

- Values that support self-expression, such as creativity, passion, authenticity.
- Values that support connection such as empathy, cooperation, collaboration.

- Values that support contribution such as service, compassion, a focus on future generations.

From the soul's perspective when you give to another you are giving to yourself. When you take care of another's needs, you are taking care of your own needs. When you connect with others, you are connecting with another aspect of yourself. The behavioral aspect of this philosophy is embedded in the golden rule which can be found in every religion. Here are three different ways the golden rule is expressed:

- One should treat others as one would like others to treat you.
- One should not treat others in ways that one would not like to be treated.
- What you wish upon yourself, you should wish upon others.

Values unite and beliefs separate

What separates us from one another are not our values; what separates us are our beliefs—the beliefs we learned in the cultural frameworks of our existence during the first 24 years of our lives. These beliefs give us our sense of identity—they tell us how we are different from other people. It is only when we get to the individuating stage of development that we begin to acknowledge our common humanity. When we individuate, we shift from belief-based decision-making to values-based decision-making. When we let go of our cultural conditioning, we begin to discover that we all share the same values.

If you have never traveled outside your country or never had a higher education—when you have never met people from other classes, races, religions or nations—you will most likely grow up with a set of beliefs that reflect your cultural heritage. In this case, you will find it hard to accept people from other classes, races, religions or nations because you will find it difficult to trust anyone who looks or behaves differently. Your beliefs will keep you separate. Only when you individuate and self-actualize will you be able to connect with other people because at those levels of consciousness we all share the same values.

3

Everything I have learned about values in my organizational life

The eight most important things I have learned about values in my organizational life are:

- To be successful, you must support your employees in meeting their needs.
- Cultural capital is the new frontier of competitive advantage.
- Organizations don't transform, people do.
- If you want to manage your culture, you must measure it.
- Regular monitoring surveys are necessary if you are serious about transforming your organization's culture.
- To build a strong culture, the leaders must create a climate of trust.
- The organization must become a trusted member of society.
- The five requirements for evolutionary leaders.

To be successful, you must support your employees in meeting their needs

Every individual in an organization, from the shop floor worker to the CEO has needs. The needs people have are a reflection of the stage of psychological development they are at and the unmet needs they have from earlier stages of development that they have not yet mastered. Whatever we need, is what we value.

Think for a moment, what is it that you need more than anything else in your working life at this point in time. Whatever it is, that is what you value.

When employees feel the organization cares about their needs—what they value—they feel a sense commitment to the organization. When they feel a sense of commitment to the organization they bring their whole selves to work. Not only that, but they also devote a significant amount of their discretionary energy to making the organization successful. Therefore, if you want to create a high-performance organization, you must develop a culture that cares about your employee's needs.

If you mostly have young employees (under 25s) in your organization, they will be focused on achievement and want respect and recognition from their manager. If you have employees in the 25 to 39 age range, they will want freedom and autonomy to test their skills and talents—to find out what they are good at, what they are not so good at, what they enjoy doing and what they don't enjoy doing. If you have employees in their forties, they will want to find meaning and purpose. They will want to express their passion and creativity through their work. If you have employees in their fifties, they will want opportunities to connect with others, to make a difference in the world. If you have employees in their sixties, they will want opportunities to contribute to the well-being of others.

In addition to respect, recognition, freedom and autonomy, many young employees these days want work that allows them to feel they can make a difference. They live in an interconnected world; they are oblivious to national, racial and religious differences. They may operate locally, but their worldview is global.

The needs that I have outlined for these different age groups, generally speaking, are true for knowledge workers—people who have had a higher education, have traveled the world and have an income that enables them to satisfy their survival, safety and security needs. These are primarily the people who have individuated and self-actualized.

For unskilled workers, labourers or those who perform clerical tasks—people who have not had a higher education, and because of the circumstances in which they live have not had the opportunity to travel (those who have not individuated and/or self-actualized), their focus, no matter what age they are at, will be on satisfying their survival, safety and security needs. They will be looking for: a) pay and benefits that enable them to support their families, b) a friendly, convivial working atmosphere, and c) opportunities to improve their skills so they can improve their prospects. They will also be interested in working overtime and getting bonuses or rewards for achieving work-related productivity targets.

Among this group will be some who want to grow and develop: who want to individuate and self-actualize. The organization should identify these people, recognize their needs and provide opportunities for them to pursue their professional *and* personal development.[8]

Cultural capital is the new frontier of competitive advantage

In 1997, when I created the Barrett Values Centre, I could already see that cultural capital was becoming the new frontier of competitive advantage. Fifteen years later, we find firms such as Deloitte, Ernst & Young and PwC issuing reports that make similar statements:

- According to E&Y[9], 55% of the FTSE[10] 350 companies have seen a 10% increase in operating profits driven by their investment in culture. Overall, 92% of the Board Members of these companies said that a focus on culture had improved their financial performance.[11]
- According to Deloitte, culture became one of the most important business topics of 2016. CEOs and HR leaders now recognize that culture drives people's behaviour, innovation, and customer service: 82% of Deloitte's survey respondents believe that "culture is a potential competitive advantage".[12]

---

[8] Richard Barrett, *The Values-Driven Organization: Cultural Health and Employee Well-Being as a Pathway to Sustainable Performance* (Routledge: London), 2017
[9] E&Y = Ernst & Young
[10] FTSE = Financial Times Stock Exchange
[11] https://go.ey.com/2s3J8dI
[12] Global Human Capital Trends 2016. The new organization: Different by design, Deloitte University Press, p. 37.

- According to PwC, 84% of leaders believe that culture is critical to their organization's success. 60% think culture is more important than their strategy or their operating model.[13]

If culture is so important to the success of an organization, it is vitally important to understand how a culture is created and how it can be measured.[14]

Organizations don't transform, people do

The culture of an organization is a reflection of the values and beliefs of the current leaders of the organization, and the institutional legacy of the values and beliefs of past leaders that have been institutionalized into the organization's structures, policies, procedures and incentives. Therefore, if you want to transform your organization's culture you must either change your leaders or your leaders must change; in addition, you must make sure the organization's structures, policies, procedures and incentives reflect the values and beliefs of the type of culture you want to create, not the values and beliefs of past leaders.

What this means is organizational transformation begins with the personal transformation of the leaders. If the leaders don't transform, the organization will not transform and the culture will remain the same.

If you want to manage your culture, you must measure it

How do you measure an organizational culture? The answer to this question is relatively simple: carry out a Cultural Values Assessment. This can be done relatively easily using the Barrett Values Centre's Cultural Transformation Tools.[15] The assessment, which takes about 10 minutes to complete, asks employees to answer three questions:

- Which of the following values/behaviours most represent who you are? (Personal Values)

---

[13] http://pwc.to/2s3JGQO
[14] See Daily Telegraph article and video at http://bit.ly/2w6KFFl
[15] Cultural Transformation Tools at http://bit.ly/2vfYGBL

- Which of the following values/behaviours most represent how your organization operates? (Current Culture)
- Which of the following values/behaviours do you believe are essential for your organization to reach its highest potential? (Desired Culture)

For each question, employees pick ten values/behaviours from a list of 80 to 90 words or phrases that have been customized for the organization. Each value/behaviour belongs to a particular level of consciousness.

When you plot the top ten votes for personal values, you know what needs employees have and what levels of consciousness they are operating from. When you plot the top ten current culture values you know the values that are being lived and the levels of consciousness the organization is operating from. When you plot the top ten desired culture values, you know what values employees believe are important for the organization to focus on and what levels of consciousness they would like to see the organization operating from.

Here are two examples. The first example presents the results of a cultural values assessment for a low-performance organization and the second presents the results of a cultural values assessment for a high-performance organization.

A low-performance organization

Figure 3.1 shows a plot of the top ten personal, current culture and desired culture values of an eighty-person organization. The diagram represents the Seven Levels of Consciousness, with survival consciousness at the bottom and service consciousness at the top; in the middle, is transformation consciousness.

Each dot on the diagram represents one of the top ten values that have been chosen by employees. An (L) after a value indicates a potentially limiting value. Positive values are shown as shaded dots and potentially limiting values are shown as white dots.

You will notice from the distribution of the top ten personal, current culture and desired culture values on the diagrams that there is a significant misalignment in consciousness between the personal values of employees (a focus at Level 5—Internal cohesion), the current culture (a focus at

Level 1—Survival and Level 2—Relationships) and the desired culture (a focus at Level 4—Transformation and Level 2—Relationships). There are no matching personal and current culture values and only one matching current and desired culture value: accountability. In a high-performance organization, we would expect to see two or three matching personal and current culture values, and five or six matching current and desired culture values.

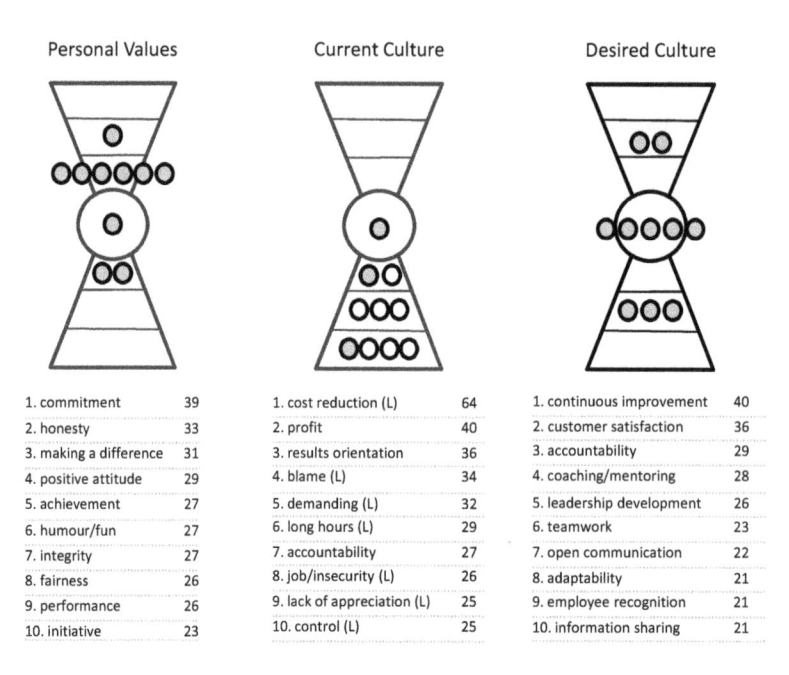

Personal Values			Current Culture			Desired Culture	
1. commitment	39		1. cost reduction (L)	64		1. continuous improvement	40
2. honesty	33		2. profit	40		2. customer satisfaction	36
3. making a difference	31		3. results orientation	36		3. accountability	29
4. positive attitude	29		4. blame (L)	34		4. coaching/mentoring	28
5. achievement	27		5. demanding (L)	32		5. leadership development	26
6. humour/fun	27		6. long hours (L)	29		6. teamwork	23
7. integrity	27		7. accountability	27		7. open communication	22
8. fairness	26		8. job/insecurity (L)	26		8. adaptability	21
9. performance	26		9. lack of appreciation (L)	25		9. employee recognition	21
10. initiative	23		10. control (L)	25		10. information sharing	21

Figure 3.1: Values plot for a low-performance organization

What is typical about this plot, which we frequently find in low-performance organizations, is a significant number of potentially limiting values in the current culture and a concentration of values at the transformation level in the desired culture. Some of the values expressed at the transformation level in the desired culture are the remedies to the issues (potentially limiting values) at Levels 1, 2 and 3 in the current culture.

The Cultural Entropy score in this organization is quite elevated at 48% and is evenly spread across Level 1—Survival (18 %), Level 2—Relationships (16%), and Level 3—Self-esteem (14%). We calculate the Cultural Entropy by adding up all the votes for potentially limiting values chosen by employees and expressing this total as a percentage of the all the votes cast.

Cultural Entropy is a measure of the internal dysfunction in an organization; it represents the amount of energy that is devoted to unproductive activities. The main source of Cultural Entropy is Personal Entropy of the leaders, managers and supervisors. The inverse of the Cultural Entropy score is an indicator of cultural health. Thus, for example, this organization has a cultural health index of 52%.

Table 3.1 shows the top value jumps in this assessment. A values jump occurs when the number of votes for a value in the current culture increases in the desired culture.

Table 3.1: Value jumps for a low-performance organization

Values	Current culture votes	Desired culture votes	Value jump
Coaching/mentoring	1	28	27
Customer satisfaction	15	36	21
Employee recognition	0	21	21
Continuous improvement	21	40	19
Open communication	21	40	19
Information sharing	4	22	17
Leadership development	10	21	16
Empowerment	3	26	16

You can see from this table that the key issue for this company is the quality of leadership. The top value jumps include coaching and mentoring, employee recognition, open communication, information sharing, leadership development and empowerment. Continuous improvement is also regarded as important by employees.

The way forward for this company

The high Cultural Entropy score and the seven potentially limiting values that show up in the top ten current culture values are a clear sign of poor performance. The focus on the bottom line (cost reduction) has caused this company to become internally focused—you will notice that customer satisfaction does not occur in the top ten values of the current culture but is the number two value in the desired culture. Additionally, there are five positive relationship values in the desired culture (accountability, open communication, coaching/mentoring, teamwork and employee recognition). These are a reaction (counterbalance) to the four potentially limiting relationship values in the current culture (blame, demanding, lack of appreciation and control).

The leaders of this organization are letting their fears dictate their behaviours. Blame, demanding, long hours, cost reduction and control are all signs that the personal entropy of the leadership group is influencing the culture of the organization. As a consequence, the company has lost its way. The organization is focused on profit, but not on customers. Neither is the company taking care of its people—lack of appreciation and job insecurity are potentially limiting values showing up in the current culture.

The values in the desired culture point the way forward: coaching/mentoring, leadership development, open communication, employee recognition and information sharing are all desired culture values that do not appear in the top ten current culture values and are high-scoring value jumps. These are the values that the leadership team needs to focus on if they want to turn this company around.

A high-performance organization

Figure 3.2 shows a plot of the top ten personal, current culture and desired culture values of a sixteen-person organization. You will notice from the distribution of the top ten personal, current culture and desired culture values on the diagrams that there is a significant alignment between the personal values of employees, the current culture and the desired culture—in each case the values are focused at Level 4 (Transformation), Level 5 (Internal cohesion) and Level 6 (Making a difference). There are four matching personal and current culture values and seven matching current and desired culture values. I have only shown nine values in the personal and current culture lists because there were several values with 4 or 7 votes respectively.

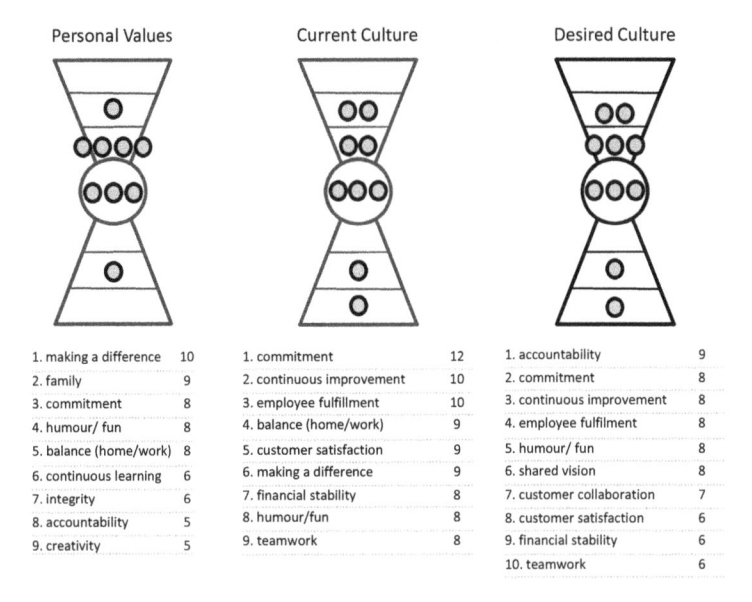

Personal Values			Current Culture			Desired Culture	
1. making a difference	10		1. commitment	12		1. accountability	9
2. family	9		2. continuous improvement	10		2. commitment	8
3. commitment	8		3. employee fulfillment	10		3. continuous improvement	8
4. humour/ fun	8		4. balance (home/work)	9		4. employee fulfilment	8
5. balance (home/work)	8		5. customer satisfaction	9		5. humour/ fun	8
6. continuous learning	6		6. making a difference	9		6. shared vision	8
7. integrity	6		7. financial stability	8		7. customer collaboration	7
8. accountability	5		8. humour/fun	8		8. customer satisfaction	6
9. creativity	5		9. teamwork	8		9. financial stability	6
						10. teamwork	6

Figure 3.2: Values plot for a high-performance organization

The cultural health index for this organization is 98% (Cultural Entropy score of 2%). This is an extremely high level of cultural health and represents a high level of employee engagement. We can conclude from these results that the employees can operate with autonomy, they find meaning and purpose in their work, and they feel like they are making a difference. It is noticeable from the values plot that there is a high degree of commitment to the organization and people enjoy their work (humour/fun).

Table 3.2 shows the top value jumps. Although the organization has a high degree of cultural health and the value jumps are quite small, there is a clear message from the employees, that the leaders should give more focus to accountability, shared vision, innovation, coaching/mentoring and leadership development.

Table 3.2: Value jumps for a high-performance organization

Values	Current culture votes	Desired culture votes	Value jump
Accountability	4	9	5
Shared vision	4	8	4
Innovation	1	5	4
Coaching/ mentoring	0	4	4
Leadership development	0	4	4

The way forward for this company

The high level of cultural health and the high number of matching personal and current culture values, and matching current and desired culture values, suggests that the leadership of this company is on the right track. Some work is needed to bring more accountability into the company and more focus needs to be given to shared vision, innovation, coaching and mentoring and leadership development.

It is important not to get complacent when you get results like this. When you take your attention away from the culture, limiting values can easily creep in. As a leader you need to be a good gardener—constantly monitoring and caring for the values of your culture.

Regular monitoring surveys are necessary if you are serious about transforming your organization's culture

When Tom Boardman was announced as CEO of Nedbank in 2003, the company was on a downward trajectory.[16] It needed the injection of a large amount of capital to keep it afloat. Tom led a series of senior management workshops to brainstorm a new strategic direction along with key focus areas and core values. Two years later Nedbank started monitoring its

---

[16] The Tom Boardman Story at http://bit.ly/2t2ILV5

values. In 2005, the Cultural Entropy score was 25%, and there were only three matching values between the current and desired culture.

By paying attention to the results of their Cultural Values Assessments, Nedbank managed to bring down the level of Cultural Entropy score to 19%, 17%, 14% and 13% over four years. By this time the number of matching current and desired culture values had risen to six. Thanks to regular monitoring, the Cultural Entropy score has stayed in the range 10% to 13%. Over the same period, the level of productivity (income per capita) has increased, and employee engagement is now at a consistently high level. Similar success stories can be found in the 25 different case studies presented on the Barrett Values Centre website.[17]

To build a strong culture, the leaders must create a climate of trust

Trust is the key to building a high performing culture. Trust begins at the top. The leaders have to be able to trust each other, and the employees have to be able to trust their leaders. Trust builds internal cohesion, increases cultural health (reduces the Cultural Entropy score) and enables the organization to build strong partnerships.

The process of building internal cohesion begins with the leadership team. The leadership team can be regarded as a cultural fractal of the whole organization. If you don't have internal cohesion in the leadership team, you will not have internal cohesion in the rest of the organization. The only way to build internal cohesion in a leadership team is to create a climate of trust.[18]

Leaders build trust when they live in alignment with their most deeply held values. Consequently, the first requirement of leaders is to know how to lead themselves—master their subconscious fears so they can live with integrity.[19]

Leaders who know how to lead themselves operate with low personal entropy. To understand the value differences between high and low entropy

---

[17] Case studies at http://bit.ly/1VqB7Md
[18] See Annex 6 (The Trust Matrix) of *The Values-Driven Organization: Cultural Health and Employee Well-Being as a Pathway to Sustainable Performance* (Routledge: London), 2017.
[19] See the website of The New Leadership Paradigm: http://bit.ly/2ttekai

leaders, we analyzed the results of 128 Leadership Development Reports[20] for leaders from 18 countries and 28 industries[21]. The data were divided into five personal entropy bands (<6%, 7 – 10%, 11 – 15%, 16 – 20%, and ≥21%).

Figure 3.3 shows the top ten values most frequently observed in leaders who are operating in the low entropy range (<6%) and the high entropy range (≥21%). Each shaded dot represents one of the values listed below the diagram—grey dots are positive values, white dots are potentially limiting values. The level of consciousness of each value is indicated in brackets.

Low Entropy Leaders <6%)

High Entropy Leaders (≥21%)

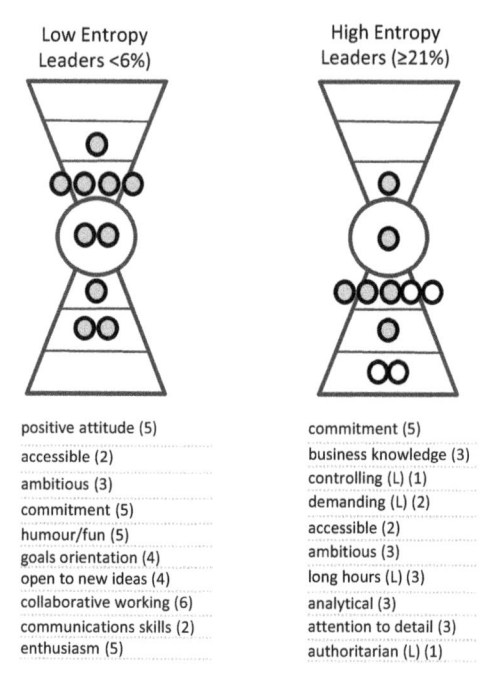

positive attitude (5)	commitment (5)
accessible (2)	business knowledge (3)
ambitious (3)	controlling (L) (1)
commitment (5)	demanding (L) (2)
humour/fun (5)	accessible (2)
goals orientation (4)	ambitious (3)
open to new ideas (4)	long hours (L) (3)
collaborative working (6)	analytical (3)
communications skills (2)	attention to detail (3)
enthusiasm (5)	authoritarian (L) (1)

Figure 3.3: Values associated with high and low personal entropy

There are three matching values between the low- and high-entropy leaders: commitment, accessible and ambitious. High entropy leaders display four potentially limiting values: controlling, demanding, long hours and authoritarian. Low entropy leaders display no potentially limiting values. High-entropy leaders feel they have to control, demand and use their power in an authoritarian way to get what they want. They also work long hours. Low-entropy leaders achieve high performance through

---

[20] For more information go to http://bit.ly/2ts8buW
[21] Fearless Leaders: http://bit.ly/2u2pcNK

collaborative working, staying open to new ideas, communicating well, bringing humour and fun to their work, being enthusiastic about what they are doing and maintaining a positive attitude.

If you compare the distribution of values for low-entropy leaders with the "values of humanity" shown in Figure 1.1, you will see the profiles are very similar: in both cases, there are a significant number of values concentrated at levels 5 and 2. This suggests that low entropy leaders tend to operate from the same levels of consciousness as humanity in general.

The organization must become a trusted member of society

If your organization wants to succeed in the twenty-first century, it will need to become a trusted member of our global society, and the leaders must become values-driven.[22] You will need to do this, not just to gain an advantage over your competitors, but to protect the investments that have been made in your company and increase its resilience. It is important to recognize that business is a wholly owned subsidiary of society, and society is a wholly owned subsidiary of the environment. If the environment fails, our society will fail and our businesses and economies will also fail.[23]

This linkage between societal well-being and business success is now well understood. Consequently, more and more leaders are looking beyond the short-term tyranny of the market place and embracing long-term sustainability. They are aligning the values of their businesses with the United Nations Sustainable Development Goals.[24]

The five requirements for evolutionary leaders

To become an evolutionary leader, there are five competencies leaders must embody adaptability, continuous learning, the ability to bond, the ability to cooperate and the ability handle complexity. If you can master these

---

[22] Richard Barrett, *The Values-Driven Organization: Cultural Health and Employee Well-Being as a Pathway to Sustainable Performance* (2nd Edition): (Routledge: London), 2017.
[23] Richard Barrett, *The New Leadership Paradigm* (Fulfilling Books: Bath), 2010.
[24] http://www.un.org/sustainabledevelopment/sustainable-development-goals/

competencies, then you will be have all the skills necessary to thrive in a volatile, uncertain, complex and ambiguous world (VUCA)[25].

What is interesting about these five competencies is that they lie at the heart of evolution. Evolution would never have happened if living entities had not been able to master these competencies.[26]

Adaptability

Adaptability is essential for thriving. It is a level 4 value. You have to be able to move with the times, go with the flow and live in the moment, if you want to survive and thrive. There are two competencies that support adaptability: agility and resilience. You have to be agile if you want to survive in a VUCA world; you also have to be resilient. You must have the strength to withstand shocks and not give up when things get tough. You must keep on transforming. Transforming is different from changing. Changing involves doing things differently; transforming requires you to adopt a new, higher order way of being—operating from a higher level of consciousness.

Continuous learning

The first 24 years of our lives are all about "emergent learning" because every new experience we have contributes to the formation of our personal belief system. It is a level 4 value. Who we are when we reach adulthood is the result of the beliefs we learned while our reptilian, limbic and neocortex mind-brains were growing and developing.

If the first 24 years of our lives were challenging—if we struggled to survive, didn't feel loved, and our accomplishments weren't recognized by our parents or peers—we will most likely have developed some limiting beliefs. These will block our future learning. We will be so preoccupied with getting our deficiency needs met, that we won't be able to individuate and

---

[25] The acronym VUCA was first used in the US Army War College to describe the state of the world after the end of the Cold War. It has been subsequently used to describe the qualities needed for strategic leadership in our modern world.

[26] See Richard Barrett, *The New Leadership Paradigm* (Fulfilling Books: Bath), 2010, for an explanation of the universal stages of evolution.

self-actualize. You have to give up your self-critical thoughts and overcome your limiting beliefs if you want to go on growing and developing. You must embrace continual learning as a way of life if you want to be an evolutionary leader.

The ability to bond

There is a famous saying: *If you want to go fast, go alone. If you want to go far, go together.* Going far—together—requires bonding. Bonding not only enables you to go far, it also enables you to go safely, because bonding with others increases everyone's resilience. There are two requirements for bonding: shared values and shared vision. Everyone must share the same ideals and must want to go in the same direction if you want to go far and go safely. The ability to bond is a level 5 value.

The ability to cooperate

When the group you have bonded with comes across an obstacle that prevents the group moving forward, you must learn to cooperate with other groups that are heading in the same direction and facing the same obstacles. Together you may be able to overcome what is blocking your way forward. Just like bonding, cooperating increases the resilience of the collective. Sometimes cooperation is so effective that groups that have successfully cooperated form a permanent higher order entity. The ability to cooperate is a level 6 value.

The ability to handle complexity

Unlike the other four competencies, the ability to handle complexity is, to a large extent, age-dependent. We can develop our adaptability, continuous learning, bonding and cooperating skills at almost any age, but our ability to handle complexity usually only develops as we reach maturity. The more experiences we have, the more knowledge we gain; the more we develop our wisdom, the abler we are to handle complexity. With wisdom comes the ability to see the big picture. We need to see the big picture to navigate complexity. The only way to do this is to expand your level of identity and awareness. Our ability to handle complexity increases as we move through the upper stages of development.

4

Everything I have learned about values in my societal life

THE SIX MOST IMPORTANT THINGS I have learned about values in my societal life are:

- We grow in stages of psychological development; we operate at levels of consciousness, and we live inside worldviews.
- The collective stages of psychological development mirror the individual stages of psychological development.
- The dominant worldview of a community/nation is a reflection of the level of consciousness the community/nation operates from.
- We can measure the level of internal cohesion (stability of the worldview of a nation) by carrying out a National Values Assessment.
- Longitudinal Values Assessments provide the possibility of monitoring changes in the social cohesion of nations.
- The evolution of human consciousness depends on the leaders of every community and nation creating the conditions that support their citizens in meeting the needs of the stage of psychological development they are at.

Stages, levels and worldviews

Every human being grows in stages of psychological development, operates at levels of consciousness and lives inside a worldview which reflects the collective stage of psychological development that the community/nation they were born into (and live in) has reached.[27] Each worldview is based on a set of values which are a reflection of the existential needs of the people.

Since the first anatomically modern humans appeared around 200,000 years ago, our species has experienced six stages of collective psychological development, each with its specific worldview. The stages of collective psychological development can be categorized by levels of identity/awareness—increasing size of human group structures.

The six levels of identity/awareness and the main focus of each worldview are shown in Table 4.1. The three shaded rows at the top of the Table 4.1 represent new levels of identity/awareness—stages of collective psychological development which will influence how communities and nations operate in future decades and centuries.[28] Although there are no nations operating from these stages of development, there are some communities and individuals operating from Humanity and Earth Awareness.

The first column of Table 4.1 lists the levels of identity/awareness. The second column describes the focus of the worldview associated with each level of identity/awareness. The third column indicates the approximate point in time when each worldview first began to appear. The fourth column shows the colour coding proposed by Ken Wilber.[29]

---

[27] I have described the seven stages of psychological development and seven levels of consciousness in Chapter 2.
[28] The structure of this model builds on the work of Clare Graves as presented in D.E Beck and C.C. Cowan, *Spiral Dynamics: Mastering values, leadership and change* (Malden: Blackwell Publishing), 2006.
[29] See http://bit.ly/2i5bVwx

Table 4.1: Levels of identity/awareness and focus of worldviews

Level of identity/ awareness	Focus of worldview	First began to appear	Colour coding
Unity Awareness	Service through contribution and compassion	n/a	Indigo
Earth Awareness	Making a difference through connection and empathy	n/a	Turquoise
Humanity Awareness	Meaning through self-expression and creativity	n/a	Teal
People Awareness	Freedom through equality and fairness	19th century	Green
World Awareness	Security through wealth and knowledge	16th century	Orange
Nation Awareness	Security through authority and education	6th century	Amber
State Awareness	Security through power and strength	4,000 BCE	Red
Tribe Awareness	Safety through belonging and loyalty	10,000 BCE	Magenta
Clan Awareness	Survival through sharing and reciprocity	Earlier than 10,000 BCE	Infrared

n/a = Not applicable. Appearing in individuals but not yet appearing to a significant extent in communities/nations.

The dates when each worldview (level of identity/awareness) first appeared refer to specific periods of history and places. It is believed that Clan Awareness and Tribe Awareness first appeared in Sub-Saharan Africa, State Awareness first appeared in North Africa, the Middle East and Central Asia, and Nation, World and People Awareness first appeared in Western Europe. In other parts of the world such as the Americas and Asia, the progression from Clan Awareness to Tribe Awareness to State Awareness occurred much later or did not happen at all. There are reasons for this which I will explain in my upcoming book *Evolutionary Dynamics* to be published in 2018. The following section provides a brief description of the characteristics and values associated with each level of identity/awareness (worldview).

The collective stages of psychological development mirror the individual stages of psychological development

I believe the collective stages of psychological development mirror the individual stages of psychological development. In other words, the values component at each stage of our collective psychological development is a direct reflection of the values component of each stage of our individual psychological development. Thus, the value system of people living in Clan Awareness—survival through sharing and reciprocity—is similar to the value system that surrounds a baby during the surviving stage of development.

Similarly, the value system of communities living in Tribe Awareness—safety through belonging and loyalty—is similar to the value system that surrounds young children at the conforming stage of development. We can also see that the value system of communities living in State Awareness, Nation Awareness and World Awareness are similar to value systems of teenagers and young adults at the three possible sub-stages of the differentiating stage of development.

Furthermore, the value system of communities living in People Awareness is similar to the value system of people at the individuating stage of development and that the value system of communities living in Humanity Awareness is similar to the value system of people at the self-actualizing stage of development. Projecting into the future, we can say the value system of communities living in Earth Awareness and Unity Awareness will be similar to the value systems of people at the integrating and serving stages of development.

Thus, in addition to using the seven stages of psychological development model to describe our individual development over a lifetime, we can also use the same model to describe the psychological development of our species. This correspondence is shown in Table 4.2.

Table 4.2: Correspondence between Levels of identity/awareness and individual stages of psychological development

Level of identity/ awareness	Focus of worldview	Individual stage of psychological development
Unity Awareness	Service through contribution and compassion	Serving
Earth Awareness	Making a difference through connection and empathy	Integrating
Humanity Awareness	Meaning through self-expression and creativity	Self-actualizing
People Awareness	Freedom through equality and fairness	Individuating
World Awareness	Security through wealth and knowledge	Differentiating
Nation Awareness	Security through authority and religious education	Differentiating
State Awareness	Security through power and strength	Differentiating
Tribe Awareness	Safety through belonging and loyalty	Conforming
Clan Awareness	Survival through sharing and reciprocity	Surviving

Based on the assumption that our collective psychological evolution is a mirror of our individual psychological evolution, we can say that the cutting-edge of our collective human journey is currently at the transition point between People Awareness (the individuating stage of development—finding freedom) and Humanity Awareness (the self-actualizing stage of development—finding meaning).[30]

The following section describes the worldviews associated with each level of identity/awareness. For each worldview, I will explain how

---

[30] In this respect, *The Rise of the Meaningful Economy*, mentioned in the Foreword, which is co-authored by Mark Drewell and Bjorn Larsson of the Foresight Group, is particularly pertinent. This publication can be accessed at www.foresight.se.

and where it originated, the dominant cosmology[31], how and where the worldview shows up today, and how the worldview relates to the individual stages of psychological development.

Clan Awareness: Survival through sharing and reciprocity.

Origins

If we assume that the species Homo sapiens first appeared about 200,000 years ago, then 95% of the life of our species has been spent in Clan Awareness. Every specimen of Homo sapiens born more than 12,000 years ago (before 10,000 BC) lived in Clan Awareness and embraced the worldview of survival through sharing and reciprocity.

During this early period of human history, people identified with small nomadic or semi-nomadic bands comprised of 20 to 30 people from 4 or 5 related families. Clans survived by hunting and gathering. They formed mutually supportive relationships with other clans operating in the same vicinity. They had very few possessions—mainly the tools they needed for survival. The practice of reciprocity, in particular, the sharing of food, was one of the ways clans helped each other to survive. There was no cultural separation in Clan Awareness and warfare was unknown.

Leadership was situational. Both sexes participated in decision-making according to the demands of the situation and the experience, knowledge and skills of the members of the clan. Men and women performed different tasks commensurate with their physical strength and their child-bearing or child-rearing activities. While men focused on hunting, women focused on gathering. Men learned the ways of animals and women learned the healing properties of plants.

There were no formal clan rules. However, there were common understandings about the spheres of activity of men and women, the support that should be given to kin, and the way in which food should be distributed. The violation of understandings was not a crime; it was more

---

[31] Cosmology: A cosmology explains our place in the universe: It describes the origin and structure of our material world, our relationship to other dimensions of existence, and most importantly, how we should conduct ourselves in regard to aligning ourselves with whomever or whatever we consider to be the "divine" creator/provider.

of an embarrassment. People's behaviours were controlled through social pressure, teasing and ridicule. There was no sense of personal ownership and no territoriality.

The cosmology of Clan Awareness

The hunter/gatherers regarded their physical environment as their home: the Earth was their "divine" mother; the world they lived in was their classroom and nature was their teacher. To them, Spirit was everywhere and in everything including themselves. Everything was connected—there was no separation. Life and death were seen as a continuum. Shamanistic practices focused on the health and well-being of the souls of the clan members: Shaman effect changes in the spirit world (energy field) which results in changes (healing) in the material world. They act as messengers between the spirit world and the human world.

How the worldview of Clan Awareness shows up today

There are very few people left on the planet who operate from Clan Awareness. They mostly live in the remote jungles of the Amazon, Papua New Guinea and Africa, and in the Aboriginal communities of Australia.

Some people suggest that the worldview of Clan Awareness can be found amongst modern day homeless people. I find this analogy misleading. Many homeless people are homeless because they are mentally disturbed: through no fault of their own they find it difficult to fit into our modern social framework. Others are homeless because they have made it a life choice: it is their way of rebelling against our modern society. Others are "travelers": members of the ethnic group known as Romani, which originated in the Northern regions of India. None of these groups of homeless people share the Clan Awareness cosmology: they do not live in a spirit world and do not conduct healing through shamanic practices. However, people in these groups may from time to time call upon their basic instincts to survive. Only, I believe, in this sense, do they operate similarly to those living in Clan Awareness.

Correspondence with the surviving stage of individual psychological development.

The worldview of Clan Awareness corresponds to the surviving stage of individual psychological development. At this stage of development, the fetus, and later the new-born baby, live in a world without separation; whatever is sensed is taken to be an extension of themselves. Everything is connected. The baby is to a large extent still living in soul consciousness. All decisions are instinctive and focused on survival. The baby, like the members of a clan, cannot survive without the sharing and caring of their kin.

Tribe Awareness: Safety through belonging and loyalty

Origins

The second worldview to emerge—safety through belonging and loyalty—is known as Tribe Awareness. This worldview first appeared around 12,000 years ago when clans expanded in size and settled in small villages. People survived through horticulture and animal husbandry. In the worldview of Tribe Awareness, people identified with an ethnic group of several hundred to several thousand people living in a specific territory.

Each tribe had its language, rituals and body adornments (dress code). Everything they "owned" belonged to the tribe. Collective aggression in this worldview was primarily limited to inter-group rivalries which showed up as occasional skirmishes and raiding. Protecting the group's food stores, animals and territory from incursions from other tribes were essential for survival. However, warfare, as we know it today, was unknown. In the worldview of Tribe Awareness people are ready to sacrifice their lives for the good of the tribe.

The worldview of safety through belonging and loyalty requires that everyone conforms to the rules of the tribe. Everything is owned by the tribe, and everything is shared—whatever "possessions" you may have belong to everyone in the tribe. Tribe Awareness operates on the principle of "Ubuntu"—a belief in a universal bond of sharing which is often translated as "I am because you are." Ubuntu consolidates the concept of reciprocity in the worldview of Tribe Awareness. You can trust people from your tribe to protect you, but you cannot trust people from other tribes.

Ceremonies and rites of passage strengthen, reinforce and stabilize people's connection to the tribe. No one is allowed to stand out and be different: individuality is suppressed. People who break the unwritten rules of the tribe are reprimanded or punished through public shaming. An apology and reparation are required before forgiveness is granted. The status of women is equal to that of men, and there are no differences in status or wealth. Elders were respected since they were regarded as the keepers of tribal wisdom.

Leaders of communities that operate from Tribe Awareness are known Big Men or Chiefs. A big man is a highly influential individual who is skilled in persuasion. He provides his followers with protection in return for gifts (usually food) which are then redistributed to members of the tribe in banquets during times of tribal festivities. This serves two functions: it keeps his followers loyal, and it consolidates his position as the big man.

The term "chief" is usually reserved for the leader of a large tribe which is stratified by social rank and maintains a permanent group of warriors paid for through some form of taxation administered by the henchmen of the chief. The chief displays his wealth and power through his dress and way of living: he lives in a big house and has many wives.

Whereas in the worldview of Clan Awareness there was no sense of separation, in the worldview of Tribe Awareness, separation shows up in the form of ethnic identity and territoriality. Differences are very important. People from other tribes are considered less than human. Therefore you can torture, maim and kill people from other tribes with abandon.

The cosmology of Tribe Awareness

People living in Tribe Awareness like those living in Clan Awareness have a strong association with the spirit world. However, because of the shift in focus from survival through sharing and reciprocity, to safety through belonging and loyalty, people living in Tribe Awareness consider kinship to be of fundamental importance and hold their ancestors in high regard. People in Tribe Awareness are bonded by blood.

Those living in the worldview of Tribe Awareness believe that after death their ancestors go on living in the spirit world and can intercede on their behalf with the Gods. Keeping the spirits of their ancestors happy is seen as a way of assuring good fortune.

Shamanic practices play an important role in the worldview of Tribe Awareness. Shamans not only know about healing using natural medicines, they also know how to mix potions to ward off evil spirits. Taboos and rituals are an important aspect of the cosmology of Tribe Awareness.

How the worldview of Tribe Awareness shows up today

The worldview associated with Tribe Awareness can still be found in large parts of Sub-Saharan Africa, in North and South America, the Caribbean and parts of Oceania. Many aspects of this worldview show up in our modern world, more specifically in the use of symbols, dress codes, superstitions, pagan and religious rituals, sports and family run businesses through to the practice of nepotism.

Correspondence with the conforming stage of individual psychological development

The young child realizes that to keep safe it must conform to the desires of the parents (which include the rules of the worldview in which the parents live). Safety depends on belonging, loyalty and staying close to your kin. The young child begins to recognize that it is living in a world of separation. It develops a separate sense of "I." This realization leads to the formation of the ego—a separate sense of self. The child's nascent ego is often suppressed by the parents for the sake of harmony in the family in the same way that individual egos are suppressed to maintain harmony in the tribe.

State Awareness: Security through power and strength

Origins

The third worldview to emerge—security through power and strength—is known as State Awareness. This worldview first appeared around 6,000 years ago (4,000 BCE) when tribes grew in size: hamlets grew into villages, villages expanded into towns and towns expanded into cities.

States ranged in size from several hundred thousand to several million citizens. Ethnicity and territory became increasingly important differentiators of identity in the worldview of State Awareness. People survived by trading, farming and animal husbandry. As the wealth of city-states grew, it became important to form a permanent army with the latest weapon technologies. To pay for the upkeep of the army, citizens were required to pay taxes.

During this stage of development, the sense of separation increased. Populations were stratified into hierarchies of power (land owners), knowledge (priests) and wealth (traders). The most powerful—those who could raise the largest army—ruled. At the bottom of the hierarchy were serfs and slaves.

Women occupied a low position in the hierarchy. They were regarded as the personal property of the father or husband and could be treated in whatever way the father or husband decided—they had no rights at all and could not hold property. This was a massive change from the two previous worldviews where women lived alongside men in a symbiotic relationship enjoying more or less equal status.

What caused this radical change was the "unleashing" of the male ego. In the preceding worldview, the ego had, to a large extent, been kept in check by the tribe. The first signs of the male ego appeared in the big man. It became more blatant later in the tribal chief. In the worldview of State Awareness, the male ego exploded—it dominated every aspect of communal life.[32]

By modern day standards, justice in State Awareness was extremely unfair. The punishment of transgressions for those in the upper strata of the hierarchy was always less severe than for those in the lower strata. If the aggressor was lower in the hierarchy than the victim, the punishment was more severe; if the aggressor was higher in the hierarchy than the victim, the punishment was less severe. An eye for an eye and a tooth for a tooth were considered normal if the aggressor and victim were at the same level in the hierarchy.

In the worldview of State Awareness, the leader had absolute power over his subjects; he was feared by those around him and considered himself above the law. No one felt safe in State Awareness. If your loyalty to the

---

[32] Steve Taylor, *The Fall: The Insanity of the Ego in Human History and The Dawning of A New Era* (Winchester Books: New York), 2005.

leader was questioned, you could be punished for treason and expect some form of immediate retribution—torture or death.

Justice was always administered through physical mutilation of the body. Death and maiming were considered suitable penalties for many infractions. To demonstrate the leader's power, punishments were administered in public and drew large crowds. Watching men fight each other to the death or being caged up with wild animals were regard as spectator sports.

Around 4,000 years ago, the ego explosion reached new heights. Instead of city-states living more or less peacefully with their neighbors, the leaders of city states started building empires: they invaded other states, plundered their riches and slaughtered their people. Those they didn't slaughter—mainly women—they captured and made into slaves to be sold in their home state to the highest bidder.

From roughly 2,000 BCE to the 6th century AD, more than 47 empires were created, most of which lasted for only 2 or 3 centuries. However, some, like the Roman Empire and the Chola Dynasty in India continued for more than 1,500 years. As a leader, you had to distribute the spoils of your empire building among your closest supporters if you wanted to keep their allegiance.

Over the next 1,500 years (from the 6th century to modern times) a further 135 empires were created. A few lasted for 500 to 800 years, but most lasted for only a few centuries.

Not all of this empire building was driven from the worldview of State Awareness. Some of the empires, particularly those created between the 6th century and the 15th century, were driven from the worldview of Nation Awareness, and others from the 16th century to the 19th century, were driven from the worldview of World Awareness. Examples of this latter group include the British Colonial Empire which lasted 394 years (from 1603 to 1997), the Spanish Empire which lasted 573 years (from 1402 to 1975), the Portuguese Empire which lasted 587 years from (1415 to 2002), the French Empire which lasted 446 years (from 1534 to 1980), and the Dutch Empire which lasted 407 years (from 1568 to 1975).[33]

---

[33] For further information on empires, consult: https://en.wikipedia.org/wiki/List_of_empires

The last empire to be created was The German Third Reich. It lasted 12 years, from 1933 to 1945. The Third Reich was driven from the worldview of State Awareness—a focus on security through power and strength.[34]

The cosmology of State Awareness

There was a significant shift in cosmology with the advent of State Awareness; a shift from reverence for the spirits of ancestors to reverence for a pantheon of Gods that "ruled" the affairs of men.

In Roman times, such Gods included Mars, the God of war, Minerva, the Goddess of Wisdom, and Neptune, the God of the sea. Everything imaginable, including all the forces of nature, had a God or Goddess in charge. Polytheism is still practiced today in traditional Chinese religion, Hinduism and Shintoism. One exception to polytheism during the era of State Awareness was the practice of Judaism—a monotheistic religion which began around 1500 BCE.

Health and healing in State Awareness were mostly focused on the use of traditional organic medicines and in intercession and sacrifices to the Gods—both animals and humans.

How the worldview of State Awareness shows up today

Leaders of nations that operate from the worldview of State Awareness demand loyalty and require constant praise and adoration. In ancient times such leaders had many wives and many offspring. In modern times, they usually have a series of "trophy" wives, to whom they are rarely faithful. Leaders operating from State Awareness constantly feed their ego's desires: they want what they want when they want it, and you had better beware if you are unable to deliver or if you cross them in any way.

They take pride in displays of military strength and accomplishment. They need such demonstrations to feed their self-esteem: they need to feel powerful, and they need to feel strong. They may even resort to displays of

---

[34] Annex 1 provides an analysis of Hitler's personality. Because of his childhood experiences, Hitler became arrested at the first sub-stage of the differentiating stage of psychological development. His need for recognition, which he never got as a child, resonated with the psyche of the German people who had been defeated in the First World War. He, and they, needed the Second World War to feed their self-esteem.

their manhood—showing off their bodies or making public appearances with beautiful women who are regarded as sexual objects. Leaders operating from the worldview of State Awareness call the shots. They will lie, cheat and manipulate to become top dog. This is the worldview of all those who use fear to manipulate others to gain power.

In the worldview of State Awareness, no leader is safe for very long. There is always someone waiting in the wings to oust the leader. For this reason, leaders in the worldview of State Awareness are extremely wary of those around them. There are intrigue and plotting everywhere. You cannot trust anyone, not even the members of your inner circle. Only the most powerful, the most fear-inducing and the most scheming leaders survive for significant periods of time. Many aspects of this worldview can be found in the Mafia, in street gangs, and in the networks of drug barons.

Leaders in this worldview have a strong interest in maintaining their physical health, having frequent sex and fathering numerous male children. Female children are less welcome. In some nations operating from the worldview of State Awareness baby daughters are murdered.

The right to bear arms is strongly defended in the worldview of State Awareness, as is the killing of wild animals and the mistreatment of domestic animals. Boxing, wrestling, bull fighting and other combat sports are all modern-day aspects of the worldview of State Awareness.

Correspondence with the differentiating stage of individual psychological development

The worldview of State Awareness corresponds to the first possible sub-stage of the differentiating stage of individual development—a focus on recognition through displays of power and strength.

The extent to which this plays out in individuals depends to a great extent on their parenting. If the children and teenagers are not nourished and cared for—not recognized by their parents for their achievements—or feel excluded from their peer group, they may resort to aggression or bullying to get their self-esteem needs met. Those who don't have a sufficient physique for fighting or bullying may take their revenge (for not being accepted and acknowledged) out on others by being manipulative and cruel, not just to the people they don't like, but also to animals. What they are trying to achieve is self-esteem through strength and superiority. What they want is to be noticed.

Nation Awareness: Security through authority and religious education

Origins

The fourth worldview to emerge—security through authority and (religious) education—is known as Nation Awareness. Nations formed when states coalesced into larger territories through alliances or the subjugation of ethnic minorities by force.

The worldview of Nation Awareness grew out of the recognition that State Awareness has four main faults: it creates chaos, instability and insecurity at the political level; it is completely focused on satisfying the needs of the male ego; it treats women as slaves, and rules the people through an ethos of fear.

The worldview of Nation Awareness brought stability, order and discipline to the governance of nations. Laws, rules and codes of conduct were established based on moral authority. Administrative bureaucracies were created to collect taxes and manage the state. Stability of leadership was achieved by the establishment of family dynasties. Kings and emperors became both political and spiritual leaders—they ruled through divine right.

Because everyone worshipped the same God, organized religion served to provide an additional bond between people of different ethnic origin living in the same nation. People who embraced a religion that was not sanctioned by the state were sometimes tolerated, often discriminated against and frequently persecuted.

Whereas in the worldview of State Awareness, elites dominated through power and strength, in the worldview of Nation Awareness, elites dominated through political and religious authority. In this worldview, everyone was answerable to God. The elites continued to rule the masses, and the masses served their needs. In return, the elites looked after the survival, safety and security of their citizens. This was the era of feudalism.

If you were one of the masses, it was difficult to improve your status in the worldview of Nation Awareness. Being of direct service to the monarch or the lord of your area, distinguishing yourself in battle or becoming a religious cleric, were the main avenues open to improving your status in society. The more loyal or righteous you became, the more your status improved.

Under the worldview of Nation Awareness, the idea of justice was modified to reflect equality in the eyes of God. Under this regime, accused persons proved their innocence by submitting to a physical ordeal, such as walking across burning coals or being doused in freezing water. It was God's will if the accused survived or not. If they survived, they were considered innocent.

In the worldview of Nation Awareness, citizens were divided into different classes—upper, middle and lower. The upper classes were represented by the monarch, his court of advisors, major land owners and religious leaders. The middle classes were represented by wealthy merchants, minor land owners and clerics. The lower classes were represented by serfs, slaves and laborers.

The cosmology of Nation Awareness

In the year AD 312 Emperor Constantine the Great of Rome had a dream about the God of the Christians the night before he went into an important battle. He won the battle and after that led the conversion of the Roman people to Christianity. This event led to a major cosmological shift—from polytheism to monotheism. Whereas the cosmology in State Awareness was based on a pantheon of Gods, the cosmology in Nation Awareness was based one God.

Several new monotheistic religions (in addition to Judaism) appeared during this period of history—Christianity and Islam being the most well-known.[35] This was the era of religious warfare. Armies were used to protect and expand religious affiliations. The concept of a "Holy War" originates from this period when Christian crusaders attempted to recapture the Holy Land from the Muslims.

Monotheistic religions teach that service to God in this life will be rewarded in the next life. Suffering and sacrifice are regarded as the pathway to everlasting life. Consequently, identification with a religion is extremely important in this worldview. Moreover, if you do not identify with *my* religion, then you are regarded as one of the heathens. This is the pathway to religious intolerance and the radicalization of believers.

---

[35] The earliest monotheistic religion was Judaism which arose in the era of State Awareness.

Health and healing in Nation Awareness are strongly focused on prayer. The body was regarded as an instrument of God. Its purpose was to do God's work. The natural impulses of the body were regarded as evil; therefore the body had to be punished for sexual thoughts. Celibacy was regarded as a pathway to God. Consequently, women were regarded as sexual temptation and their bodies had to be hidden from view. Sexual union between men and women had to be consecrated in the eyes of God. Homosexuality was forbidden.

How the worldview of Nation Awareness shows up today

The leaders of nations operating from Nation Awareness regard themselves as the ultimate authority. Consequently, they significantly influence and meddle with the affairs of state and the justice system—they intervene to grant pardons to those condemned to death.

In the worldview of Nation Awareness, the mixing of social classes is frowned upon as is the union in marriage of men and women from different ethnic or religious groups. Belonging to the correct ethnic and religious group is extremely important. Belonging to the wrong ethnic or religious group can jeopardize your safety. This worldview spawned white and black supremacists, as well as the Ku Klux Klan and Neo-Nazi political movements. In the worldview of Nation Awareness, women are second-class citizens and have much less freedom than men. Homophobia is rife in the worldview of Nation Awareness.

Group structures in the worldview of Nation Awareness are governed though hierarchies of authority—the civil service, the military and organized religions. You advance your position through sacrifice, self-discipline and loyalty. Rarely do people get promoted for their abilities; your pathway to authority involves decades of service with a promise of a pension at the end. A central tenet of the worldview of Nation Awareness is sacrifice now for rewards later. Higher positions, awards and decorations are reserved for those who have supported the leaders in some significant way or have shown outstanding service to the nation.

In the worldview of Nation Awareness leaders consider it acceptable to use the machinery of Government to satisfy their personal desires. They use their influence to grant favours to those who are loyal or wield significant power—money and political power go hand in hand.

Leaders believe they can operate outside the law. They tend to manipulate the masses through fear. They seek ways to change the laws to allow them to stay in power for longer periods of time than the constitution currently allows. In this worldview, religion can play a significant role in the formation of political alliances. Education systems in this worldview strongly emphasize religious knowledge.

Correspondence with the differentiating stage of psychological development

The worldview of Nation Awareness corresponds to the second possible sub-stage of the differentiating stage of individual development—a focus on recognition through authority and (religious) education. If teenagers are cared for and recognized for their achievements by their parents and respected by their peers, instead of seeking recognition through power, they may seek recognition through authority—focusing on their studies to gain more respect from their parents, authority figures or peers.

I would like to include an important caveat regarding this point. When a community embraces the worldview of Nation Awareness, but the parents do not take sufficient care of their teenager's needs—do not recognize them for their achievements—the teenagers (mainly males but also some females) may turn to religious authority figures to get the recognition they are seeking. This may cause them to deepen their relationship with their religion. In the wrong hands, they become ripe for radicalization by religious extremists. This is true for all monotheistic religions: Christian, Islam and Judaism.

World Awareness: Security through wealth and knowledge

Origins

The fifth worldview to emerge—security through wealth and knowledge—is known as World Awareness. This worldview began to appear in the fifteenth century when the most powerful nations of Europe began to dispatch their navies to explore distant lands—empire-building to build wealth. The Portuguese, Spanish, French, Dutch and British competed with each other to colonize the Americas, the Caribbean, Africa and the East Indies to gain wealth through trade.

The worldview of World Awareness grew out of the recognition that Nation Awareness has four main faults. Nation awareness discriminates against ethnic and religious differences; it treats women as second-class citizens, it is extremely homophobic, and it gives too much power and influence to leaders of religious institutions.

In World Awareness, the governance structures of nations began to shift from the absolute power of Kings, Queens or religious leaders to constitutional monarchies. Monarchs began to give up their powers to elected representatives of the people. For the most part, these were males—people from the (rich) upper classes, important land owners or recognized public figures. During the worldview of World Awareness, the power of the aristocracy began to slowly wane as the concept of democracy began to take hold.

The first democracies to appear were either single party systems (in the case of nations dominated by religious leaders) or two-party systems in nations dominated by secular leaders—one party representing the conservative elites attempting to cling to their privileges and power, and one party representing liberal thinkers or the working classes seeking to get a fairer share of the wealth they were creating through their labours.

As far as women were concerned, the era began in the worst possible way. The male-dominated religious institutions exerted their power over women by labeling anyone who was suspected of evil or malicious behaviours as a witch. Women healers and shaman were particularly targeted. It is estimated that more than 200,000 witches were put to death in the 16th, 17th and 18th centuries in Europe.

The idea of natural justice (by God), which was present in Nation Awareness, was replaced by the idea of rational justice (by men) administered by high ranking elites. In the early era of World Awareness, torture was considered an appropriate method of extracting the truth. It was rare that court proceedings lasted more than a few days. Once a sentence had been passed, the punishment was instantaneous. Punishment was administered by the beating or mutilating the wrongdoer's body. What we would consider today as minor crimes, were punished by violent death: being burnt alive or being hung, drawn and quartered in public. Minor offenses were punished by placing criminals in public stocks where citizens could humiliate them.

Public humiliation continued to be a means of punishment until the arrival of the worldview of People Awareness in the 19th century.

The cosmology of World Awareness

During the era of the worldview of World Awareness, science replaced religion as the dominant cosmology. Healing through medicine, rather than through prayer became the norm. Consequently, in the worldview of World Awareness, the cosmology of religion based on one "true" God was replaced by the cosmology of science. In science, there is *no* God—no divine creator/provider, *no* soul, *no* other dimensions of existence, and therefore no life after death. The concept of Darwinian meaninglessness—evolution based on random mutations—became accepted as the foundation of evolution. In the worldview of World Awareness, Atheism became popular.

Whereas all previous cosmologies could be classified as transcendent—the extension of consciousness into other dimensions of existence—science was non-transcendent. This shift from a transcendent cosmology (an external God) to science (a non-transcendent cosmology), significantly affected academia, particularly the humanities, more specifically, the domains of philosophy and psychology. The soul, which at first was regarded by some as a legitimate concept in psychology, under the influence of science was gradually replaced by behavioural psychology.

Health and healing in the worldview of World Awareness are based on science. The body is treated as a machine, and psychological problems are treated by drugs. Physicians ignore any linkages between the mind and the body.

How the worldview of World Awareness shows up today

World Awareness arose during colonial times when people from different countries were able to travel and settle in other countries. Thus, we began to see a growing diversity of ethnic populations settling in the former colonial nations. For example, the UK integrated people from the West Indies, Pakistan, India and East Africa. France integrated people from West, North and Sub-Saharan Africa as well as Vietnam. The Netherlands integrated people from Indonesia, Spain integrated people from South America, and Portugal integrated people from Brazil and Mozambique. While integrating people of different ethnicities into societies operating from World Awareness is not too difficult, integrating them into societies operating from Nation Awareness, where identity is more important, can be very problematical.

In the worldview of World Awareness politics tend to be polarized into two main parties: one party usually represents the affluent and privileged and the other party usually represents the poor, less well-off and the under privileged.

In World Awareness, the rich and powerful try to influence political decision-making through bribery and corruption. The poor and the disadvantaged, and the environment, seldom win out in communities and nations dominated by World Awareness: making money is paramount. The gap between the rich and poor grows wider because those with wealth invest their money at interest rates that are higher than the rate of increase of incomes. Thus, those without wealth gradually get left behind.

The work of women is not as highly valued as the work of men, even when they have equivalent qualifications. Consequently, women find it more difficult to reach positions of influence in nations operating from World Awareness.

World Awareness spawns young entrepreneurs—people who use their intelligence to create products and services that they believe will make them rich. The focus of education in World Awareness is to prepare people to compete with each other in the world of work. Consequently, many young people sign up for universities where they can get an MBA—a Master Degree in Business Administration. The underlying cosmology in World Awareness is science: there is no God and no soul in science.

Correspondence with the differentiating stage of psychological development

The worldview of World Awareness corresponds to the third possible sub-stage of the differentiating stage of individual development—a focus on recognition through wealth and knowledge. For the non-elites living in this worldview, knowledge through formal education is the most direct pathway to wealth. Intelligence and being smart are highly-valued at this particular sub-stage of development, as is success, fame and status. Competition is the norm. Achievement means everything.

Richard Barrett

People Awareness: Freedom through equality and fairness

Origins

The sixth worldview to emerge—freedom through equality and fairness—is known as People Awareness. This worldview first began to appear in Europe in the 19th century.

The worldview of People Awareness grew out of the recognition that World Awareness had three main drawbacks. It created rampant inequality; it was bad for the environment; and it discriminated against women, homosexuals and transgender people.

People Awareness attempted to correct the imbalances between the elites (the rich) and the masses (the poor) that had been present in human societies since the explosion of the male ego more than 6,000 years ago.

Consequently, the worldview of People Awareness represented a major transformation in our collective psychological development. Central to this worldview is the concept of inclusivity. This was achieved through equality and the "demonization" of privilege—an aspect of elitism which was present in State Awareness, Nation Awareness and World Awareness. Our collective psychological development was beginning to tame the male ego.

Around the beginning of the 20th century women were allowed to vote, and a few decades later they were allowed to stand for election. Under the aegis of democracy, the influence of the aristocracy and wealthy elites continued to wane. Class systems began to dissolve, and universal education became the norm. At a geopolitical level, former colonies were granted independence and given equal status in the United Nations.

The acceptance of diversity through inclusivity also fueled other changes, such as the recognition of the rights of indigenous peoples. In addition, nations operating from the worldview of People Awareness gladly accepted refugees who were being discriminated against in nations rooted in State or Nation Awareness.

Under the aegis of the worldview of People Awareness, slavery was abolished (in the early 19th century), and the justice system was completely revamped. For example, in the UK, the number of offenses which demanded the death penalty was reduced from over 200 to around five. Executions were now carried out privately in prisons rather than being public spectacles.

Instead of taking vengeance on the body, the new system of justice punished people's "souls."[36] Incarceration became the primary mode of punishment. The more serious the crime, the longer was your detention. Instead of punishment being regarded as a form of retribution as in Nation Awareness, and a form of deterrence as in World Awareness, it became regarded as an opportunity to focus on rehabilitation—helping people who have broken the law to reintegrate into society. No matter how serious your crime, in People Awareness there is no capital punishment.

The nations where the worldview of People Awareness first took root where those that had only marginally participated in the colonial land grab in the era of World Awareness—because of this, these nations had remained, to a large extent, ethnically homogenous. Thus, while the ex-colonial powers operating from World Awareness were struggling with diversity issues caused by the influx of peoples from their former colonies, the ethnically homogenous nations—mostly Scandinavian and those that were less successful colonizers—made strides in the domains of gender, sexual and social integration.

Everyone's voice and everyone's aspirations are considered important in People Awareness. The primary mode of decision-making in this worldview became consensus: conflicts were avoided, and dialogue was considered important before a decision could be made.

The cosmology of People Awareness

People Awareness heralded a major cosmological shift. Whereas in Nation Awareness we worshipped an external God and in science we worshipped no God, in People Awareness we began to form a relationship with the God inside us—our own personal God—we embraced spirituality.

Spirituality unites people from different faiths by focusing on the values that people share rather than the beliefs that separate them. In addition to promoting equal treatment of people of different religions, People Awareness promoted the equal treatment of different genders, sexual orientation and race. There are no barriers to sexual unions in People Awareness. Despite the objections of male religious clerics (most

---

[36] Michel Foucault, *Discipline and Punish: The Birth of the Prison* (London: Penguin Books), 1977.

operating from Nation Awareness), same-gender marriages became legal, and women were gradually accepted into the priesthood.

The principal problem with spirituality in the worldview of People Awareness is that it is only one step removed from the ego dominance we find in the worldview of World Awareness. Consequently, spirituality is easily high-jacked by well-educated people seeking fame and fortune as spiritual gurus. They used their knowledge of the spiritual world to make personal fortunes utilizing the vehicle of the self-help movement. These are the people who are moving into the individuating and self-actualizing stage of psychological development, who have given up on organized religions and are seeking to connect with their God within.

Health and healing in the worldview of People Awareness is strongly orientated towards alternative, non-invasive natural medicine and spiritual therapies that focus on mind-body integration. The modalities of mindfulness and meditation are regarded as having beneficial effects on the mind and the body in this worldview.

How the worldview of People Awareness shows up today

Governments in nations operating with People Awareness are often made up of coalitions, reflecting the diverse priorities of citizens. Men and women are treated equally, and people with different sexual orientations are accepted. There is no discrimination of any type in People Awareness. In this worldview political correctness—the avoidance of language or actions that exclude, marginalize or insult groups of people who are seen as disadvantaged or different—is the sine-qua non for proper relations. Everyone's feelings are respected. Consensus is important because disharmony and emotional outbursts are to be avoided in this worldview.

In the worldview of People Awareness we begin to see a shift in emphasis in education from reading, writing and arithmetic—the skills required to support the economy (preparing children for the worldview of World Awareness)—to values-based education, preparing children for the worldview of People Awareness.[37] Significant attention is also given to the needs of animals—domestic and wild. Socialized medicine, alternative medicine and financial safety nets are available to all in this worldview. The underlying cosmology in People Awareness is spirituality.

---

[37] http://www.valuesbasededucation.com/

Correspondence with the individuating stage of psychological development

The worldview of People Awareness corresponds to the individuating stage of personal development—a focus on freedom and autonomy. At this stage of development, you begin to discover who you are outside your parental and cultural conditioning. You become responsible and accountable for your life. You start to let go of your dependency on others and institutions to meet your deficiency needs. You begin to face your fears.

Honesty, openness and transparency are key values at the individuating stage of development. Instead of making decisions based on your beliefs, you begin to make decisions based on your values. Your values become your internal guidance system for making decisions.

Humanity Awareness: Meaning through self-expression and creativity

Origins

The worldview now emerging—the seventh—is known as Humanity Awareness. Whereas this worldview can be found in some individuals and a few communities, there are as yet no nations operating from this worldview.

Humanity Awareness is the first worldview that is truly systemic and integral. It takes decision-making to a new level—it looks at the big picture considering the whole rather than the parts—it focuses on the needs of our global society. It represents an even greater transformation in our collective psychological development than People Awareness.

Unlike previous worldviews, the humanity worldview sees the "verticality" of societal development—understands the evolutionary perspective. People operating from the first six worldviews are unable to step into the shoes of those operating with other worldviews: they look at the world through the myopic beliefs of their worldview. They are unable to embrace the concept of cultural evolution because they live in societal flatland—they look out at the world and judge it from their worldview. For example, those operating from the worldview of Nation Awareness see those operating from the worldview of People Awareness as "bloody" liberals, and those operating from the worldview of People Awareness see those operating from the worldview of Nation Awareness as homophobic racists.

People operating from the worldview of Humanity Awareness see other worldviews not through the lens of competing beliefs structures but through the lens of value priorities. They see the verticality of consciousness—people at different stages of psychological development have different needs. In the worldview of Humanity Awareness, the evolution of human consciousness is seen as a work in progress.

In Humanity Awareness, chaos and change are seen as natural. Difficulties are regarded as opportunities for learning, rather than problems to be solved. People with this worldview may get anxious about the future, but they are not fearful. They trust in their collective knowledge and creativity to resolve all issues.

Respect and recognition in Humanity Awareness are earned; it is not dependent on power, authority or wealth. Leadership is situational; it is based on a person's level of competence and creativity.

Justice in Humanity Awareness recognizes that people make mistakes due to their childhood conditioning. Rehabilitation is handled though psycho-therapeutic support (the reprogramming of limiting beliefs) and self-knowledge—understanding your true nature.

Humanity Awareness heralds a new form of democracy, not dominated by power, authority, and status hungry elites, but by citizens working together collaboratively to find solutions which focus on the good of the whole. In this worldview, discord is not shied away from. It is seen as an opportunity for people to grow and develop. The differences between political parties become marginal. Decision-making is decentralized to the appropriate regional or local level.

To tackle issues such as the pollution of the global commons, global warming, and international crime, a new global governance system begins to develop based on national representation at a regional level, and regional representation at a global level.[38] The United Nations is completely overhauled or disappears.

Humanity Awareness also heralds a new approach to education. Values-based education becomes the norm. Also, children are taught from

---

[38] Richard Barrett, *Love, Fear and the Destiny of Nations* (Fulfilling Books: Bath), 2011.

a young age how to manifest their soul's self-expression, how to connect with other souls, and how to contribute to the common good of humanity.

Health and healing in the worldview of Humanity Awareness is energetically-based. It is focused on ego-soul alignment. The body is seen as an energy field—the vehicle of the soul in the material dimension of existence. When the energy field is healthy—aligned with the motivations of the soul—the body is healthy.[39]

The cosmology of Humanity Awareness

Whereas the cosmology of People Awareness united people of different religions through an awareness of values, the worldview of Humanity Awareness unites all peoples of the planet—people of different ethnicity, nationality, race and gender—in an overarching cosmology that unifies the belief systems of spirituality, science and psychology in an energetic framework of understanding, where every human being is recognized as an individuated aspect of the universal energy field—as an energetic soul experiencing three-dimensional reality in a physical body. In other words, everyone on the planet shares the same sense of identity and shares the same humanitarian values. There are no forms of discrimination in Humanity Awareness. There is a common understanding that when I give to you, I give to another aspect of myself.

Correspondence with the self-actualizing stage of psychological development

The worldview of Humanity Awareness corresponds to the self-actualizing stage of personal development—a focus on internal cohesion (ego-soul alignment) and external cohesion—through shared vision and shared values. People operating from this level of consciousness are looking to express their soul's purpose. They want to become whole. They want to bond with other people in group structures that care about the future of humanity.

---

[39] Richard Barrett, *A New Psychology of Human Well-Being: An Exploration of the Influence of Ego-Soul Dynamics on Mental and Physical Health* (Fulfilling Books: London), 2016.

Beyond Humanity Awareness

Beyond Humanity Awareness lie two, as yet nascent levels of identity/awareness—Earth Awareness and Unity Awareness. Earth Awareness recognizes that all living organisms on the planet are interconnected in an energetic web of life. They are individuated aspects of the "Gaia"[40] energy field—every living thing is dependent on the energy field of the Earth for its continuing existence. Unity Awareness goes beyond individuated energetic awareness. At this level of awareness, we recognize that we are at one with everything. There is no longer any separation whatsoever. We can transcend our three-dimensional material awareness and our four-dimensional energetic awareness and see the world we live in through the eyes of unity consciousness.

Earth Awareness: Making a difference through connection and empathy

Whereas the task in the worldview of Humanity Awareness was to bond with yourself—fully align your ego with your soul—the task in the worldview of Earth Awareness is to connect and collaborate with every other human soul for the purpose of nurturing humanity and safeguarding our home—the planet. We return to our evolutionary roots and become a new tribe—a tribe of souls caring for all other souls, and caring for the soul of the planet. The ego fears have practically disappeared and no longer influence our decision-making.

At the personal level we learned in the worldview of People Awareness to live according to a shared set of values, and in the worldview of Humanity Awareness we learned how to identify our gifts and talents. In the Earth worldview, we learn how to cooperate with others to use our collective gifts and talents to co-create a new world. We cannot do it on our own; we can only do it together. There is a common understanding at this level of awareness that we are the ones the world has been waiting for.

We see ourselves and the world we live in as a complex energy system. Our job is to balance our collective energies (the energy field of humanity),

---

[40] Gaia refers to the Earth as a self-regulating complex system which includes all life forms.

so we are in tune (resonate) with the energy field of the planet. To make this happen, we must work where the energies are the least balanced—where there is most fear—in the nations that are struggling to meet their basic needs, where people have not yet developed full self-awareness. In this sense, the UN Sustainable Development goals are seen as a good start in manifesting this level of Identity/Awareness.

In the worldview of Earth Awareness we return to a communal worldview, like that of Tribe Awareness; not as different ethnic communities, but as a global tribe of souls—everyone an individuated aspect of the soul of the human species—living inside the individuated aspect of the universal energy field we call the Earth.

We return to a communal worldview not as spirits but as beings of energy. The task at this stage of development is for each person to reintegrate energetically with the energy field of humanity and for the energy field of humanity to reintegrate with the energy field of the planet. This impulse is already showing up in the drive towards sustainable ecological development at the planetary level.

People operating with this worldview understand holism. They see the embedded nature of things; they see individuals embedded in families, which in turn are embedded in communities. They see communities and organization embedded in nations, which in turn are embedded in the living organism we call Earth. They see the interconnectedness of all things. They look at the world and see the interplay of forces and energies. They understand how all the other worldviews operate and integrate.

The energetic connection between souls is felt, and each soul has access to what Carl Jung called the collective unconscious—the storehouse of knowledge available in the universal energy field of humanity. Thoughts are shared at this level of consciousness without speaking.

Your soul thoughts drive your decision-making—this is known as inspiration. Your intuition and inspiration guide everything you do. You are a soul with an energy field that manifests in three-dimensional material awareness as a body. The energy field is your only reality.

Unity Awareness: Service through contribution and compassion

We return now to undifferentiated wholeness as we learn to operate from the highest level of Human Awareness: the quantum level of existence.

We understand that our collective beliefs create our collective reality and personal beliefs create our personal reality. We are the co-creators of the world we experience.

At this level of awareness, we immerse ourselves in the experience of being. There is no focus on past or future, and there is a complete absence of separation. Subject and object merge into one. We live in a state of non-duality. It is difficult to say much more about Unity Awareness because it has to be experienced. Words cannot do justice to this level of being.

Conclusions

There are three important conclusions which come from the understanding of the evolution of worldviews described in the preceding paragraphs:

1. Every advance in worldviews corresponds to a higher level of social integration—more inclusivity, less separation.
2. Every advance in worldviews corresponds to a higher level of social complexity as human group structures become progressively larger and more ethnically diverse.
3. Every advance in social complexity demands a higher level of mind functioning and a higher level of soul integration. Only the soul can operate from the higher levels of identity/ awareness.

The dominant worldview of a community/nation is a reflection of the level of consciousness the community/nation operates from

Based on the foregoing, we can state that the worldview embraced by a democratic community/nation is a reflection of the stages of collective psychological development that the majority of the population is operating from, and that the worldview embraced by an autocratic regime is a reflection of the stages of individual psychological development that the leader of the regime is operating from.

In the very near future, I propose to develop a survey instrument to measure the dominant worldviews in a community or nation. In the meantime, I have developed a more generalized method. I call it the Global

Consciousness Indicator (GCI)—a way of ranking nations by their relative levels of consciousness.

I created the GCI for nations by identifying two or three existing global indicators for each of the Seven Levels of Consciousness. For example, I used the Peace Index as one of the indicators for the relationship level of consciousness, and I used the Democracy Index as one of the indicators for the transformation level of consciousness. In total, I used 17 indicators to determine the GCI for 145 nations. I normalized the data for each set of global indicators—the top score was given 100 points and the bottom score 0 points—to obtain an average score for each level of consciousness and then added up the scores to obtain an overall score for each nation.

In order to check the validity of the results, I compared the GCI ranking of nations with the Happiness Indicator (HI) ranking of nations.[41] I obtained a correlation coefficient 0.7189 indicating a moderate to strong positive correlation between the Happiness Indicator and the Global Consciousness Indicator. Figure 4.1 shows the plot of GCI ranking against HI ranking. The correlation between the HI and GCI ranking is especially significant in the most developed nations. What this is saying is that highest ranking nations in consciousness terms are also the highest ranking nations in happiness terms: there is a symbiotic relationship between consciousness and happiness.

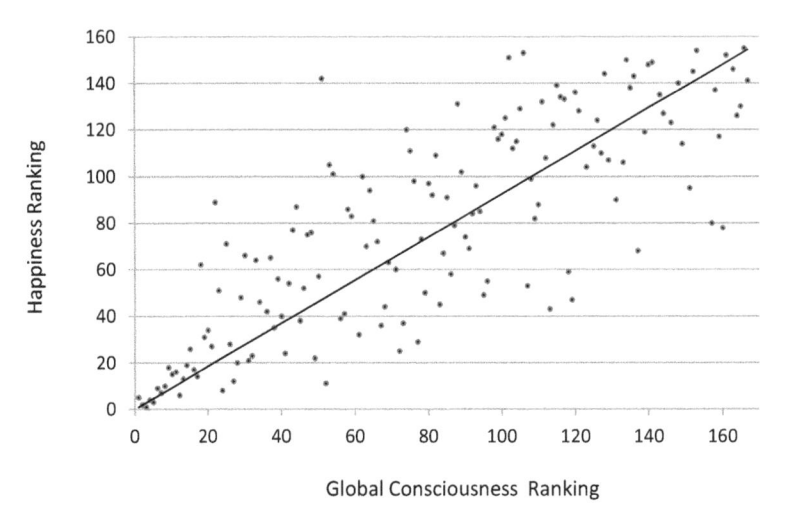

Figure 4.1: HI rankings vs. GCI rankings

---

[41] World Happiness Report at http://bit.ly/2r8zLe9

I then did a second correlation. I compared the GCI rankings with the GAPFRAME (GF) rankings of the Business School of Lausanne. The GAPFRAME translates the seventeen UN Sustainable Development Goals into nationally relevant issues and indicators showing where a country is today compared to its ideal future state.[42] The highest ranking nations are those that have the smallest gap between where they are and the SDG. I obtained a correlation coefficient 0.8440 indicating a moderate to strong positive correlation between the Global Consciousness Indicator and the GAPFRAME Indicator.

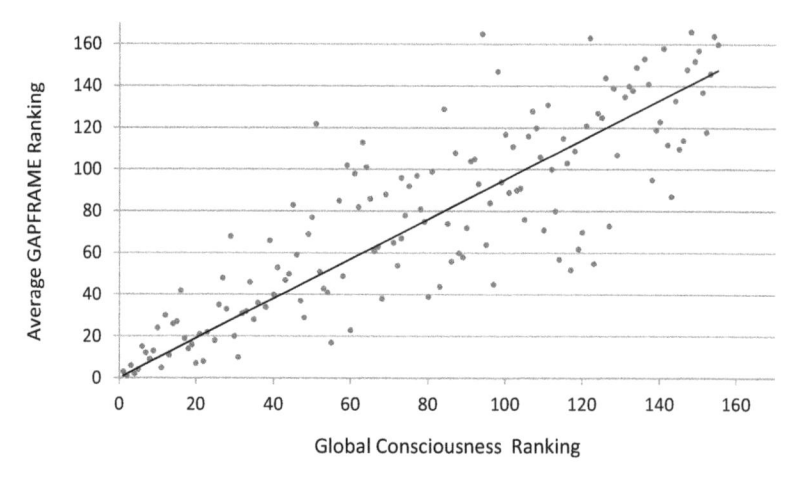

Figure 4.2: GF rankings vs. GCI rankings

The correlation between the GCI and GF ranking is especially significant in the most developed nations. What this is saying is that highest ranking nations in consciousness terms are also the highest ranking nations in the implementation of the UN's Sustainable Development Goals. In other words, there is a symbiotic relationship between consciousness and sustainability.

These moderate to strong positive correlations between consciousness and happiness, and consciousness and sustainability suggest that as consciousness evolves, the general well-being of humanity improves.

Having reassured myself that the GCI rankings show a high level of correlation with the rankings of other consciousness related data sets, I

---

[42] http://gapframe.org/

used the Global Consciousness Indicator scale as a proxy to determine the predominant worldviews of 145 nations.

I considered the highest ranking nations to be operating from People Awareness. These nations are Finland, Norway, Denmark, Switzerland, Sweden, Iceland and New Zealand.

I considered the next group to be operating from World Awareness. These nations are Canada, Australia, Luxembourg, Ireland, The Netherlands Germany, Austria, the United Kingdom and Belgium.

Because the GCI scores represent a spectrum of consciousness, we can consider nations at the top of a grouping to be close to operating from the next emergent worldview and those at the bottom of the grouping to be close to operating from the previous worldview. Thus, for example, Canada can be considered close to operating from the worldview of People Awareness.

I considered the next group to be operating from Nation Awareness. These nations include the US, Singapore, Slovenia, France, Spain, Malta, Portugal, Japan, New Zealand, Costa Rica, Uruguay, Estonia, Chile and Italy. The US, Singapore and Slovenia can be considered close to operating with World Awareness and Estonia, Chile and Italy can be considered close to operating with State Awareness.

I considered the next group to be operating from State Awareness. I split this group into three bands. The upper band represents those nations that are moving towards Nation Awareness. At the top of this band are the Cyprus, Mauritius and Poland.

The middle band of State Awareness includes nations such as Thailand, Vietnam and Indonesia in the Far East, Colombia, Ecuador and Peru in South America, and Tunisia, Turkey and Morocco in the Middle East. In this middle sub-band, we also find nations operating with a substrate of Tribe Awareness, such as Ghana, Zambia, Gabon, Rwanda, Kenya, Senegal and Tanzania,.

The lower band also includes some Sub-Saharn African nations as well as Iran, India, Egypt Bangladesh, Afghanistan and North Korea.

While these classifications of worldview, based on relative levels of consciousness may not be precise, I believe they provide a very insightful "vertical" lens through which we can view the evolution of consciousness of nations.

Measuring the level of internal cohesion by carrying out a National Values Assessment

Nations experience high levels of internal cohesion—low Cultural Entropy scores—to the extent that the majority of people share the same worldview and the leaders enable the citizens to live in alignment with that worldview; in other words, the leader or the leaders of a nation create the conditions that enable the majority of the people to get their needs met at the stage of psychological development they are at.

We can measure the degree to which a nation is aligned with its dominant worldview by using the Cultural Transformation Tools to carry out a National Values Assessment and measure the Cultural Entropy score. A low Cultural Entropy score means the people are aligned with the dominant worldview—a high level of internal cohesion. A high Cultural Entropy score indicates a low level of alignment with the dominant worldview—a low level of internal cohesion.

Table 4.3 shows the Cultural Entropy scores for 25 nations where the Barrett Values Centre has carried out National Values Assessments (between 2007 and 2017). For those nations marked with an asterisk (*) several National Values Assessments have been carried out. The years in which these assessments were made and Cultural Entropy score that was measured, are shown at the foot of Table 4.3.

You will see from Table 4.3 that Denmark (2008), Switzerland (2011), Bhutan (2007) and the United Arab Emirates (UAE) (2012) all have a relatively low Cultural Entropy scores (less than 30%), indicating a strong level of social cohesion—alignment with the dominant worldview. The next group of most aligned nations, with Cultural Entropy scores less than 40% and more than 29%, include Sweden (2009 and 2010), Canada (2010), Singapore (2015), Australia (2016) and the Kingdom of Saudi Arabia (KSA) (2016).

The next group (misaligned nations), with Cultural Entropy scores in the range 40% to 60% include Iceland (2008 and 2010), Sweden (2011 to 2017), UK (2012), USA (2009 and 2011), Latvia (2007), Brazil (2010), Nigeria (2012), Slovakia (2016) and Turkey (2016). The most misaligned nations, with a Cultural Entropy score above 60% were Iceland (2016), Italy (2012), South Africa (SA) (2011), France (2013 to 2016), Venezuela (2009), Trinidad and Tobago (2102) and Hungary (2012).

Table 4.3: Levels of identity/awareness (worldviews) and Cultural Entropy scores in 25 nations

People Awareness	World Awareness
Denmark 21% (2008)	Canada 32% (2010)
Iceland* 54% (2008)	UK 59% (2012)
Switzerland 26% (2011)	Belgium 53% (2010)
Finland* 49% (2011)	Singapore* 37% (2015)
Sweden* 46% (2017)	Australia 39% (2016)

Nation Awareness	State Awareness
USA* 56% (2011)	Bhutan 4% (2007)
Italy 73% (2012)	Latvia 54% (2007)
France* 65% (2016)	Venezuela 72% (2009)
	Brazil 51% (2010)
	SA 62% (2011)
	Trinidad 75% (2012)
	Hungary 82% (2012)
	Nigeria 57% (2012)
	UAE 12% (2012)
	KSA 34% (2016)
	Slovakia 59% (2016)
	Turkey 52% (2016)

* In the countries with an asterisk Cultural Values Assessments have been carried for two years or more.

- Iceland 43% (2010), 61% (2016)
- Finland 48% (2010), 49% (2012)
- France 57% (2012), 65% (2013), 65% (2014), 61% (2015)
- Singapore 41% (2012)
- Sweden 31% (2009), 34% (2010), 42% (2011), 43% (2012), 47% (2013), 43% (2014), 47% (2016)
- USA 52% (2009)

Until recently, I had wrongly assumed that the most democratic nations would have the highest levels of social cohesion and lowest Cultural Entropy score. Thus I found it difficult explain why Iceland in 2008 had a 52% Cultural Entropy score and the UAE in 2012 had only a 12% Cultural Entropy score. According to the Economic Intelligence Unit's Democracy Index, Iceland ranked #2 in the world regarding democracy in 2008 and UAE ranked #147 in 2012. I therefore expected the people of Iceland to have a higher level of social cohesion than the people of the UAE. In fact, the reverse was true.

This was when I realized that Cultural Entropy is a function of the degree to which the majority of the people of a nation are currently aligned with the dominant worldview. The lack of internal cohesion in Iceland—with an elevated Cultural Entropy score—was a sign that the majority of the people in Iceland felt that the current culture of the nation was not in alignment with the dominant worldview (People Awareness). On the other hand, the strong level of internal cohesion in the UAE—with a low Cultural Entropy score—was a sign that the current culture of the nation was in alignment with the dominant worldview (State Awareness). This was just as true for males as females in the UAE: males had a Cultural Entropy score of 12% and females 11%.

When I visited Iceland in September 2008 to present the results of the National Values Assessment, I stated that if Iceland were an organization with this level of Cultural Entropy, it would soon go bankrupt. Two weeks later, Iceland went bankrupt. What was causing the high Cultural Entropy score in Iceland was the values and behaviours of the leaders: the bankers and the leading politicians.

Iceland assessment

Figure 4.3 shows the results of the National Values Assessment for Iceland carried out in 2008. Six hundred and thirty-five people participated in this statistically valid survey. Table 4.3 shows the value jumps for Iceland.

EVERYTHING I HAVE LEARNED ABOUT VALUES

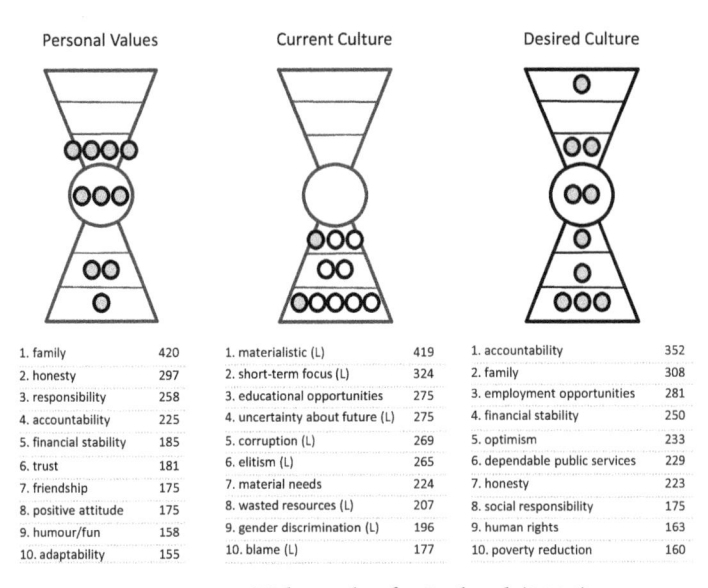

Personal Values		Current Culture		Desired Culture	
1. family	420	1. materialistic (L)	419	1. accountability	352
2. honesty	297	2. short-term focus (L)	324	2. family	308
3. responsibility	258	3. educational opportunities	275	3. employment opportunities	281
4. accountability	225	4. uncertainty about future (L)	275	4. financial stability	250
5. financial stability	185	5. corruption (L)	269	5. optimism	233
6. trust	181	6. elitism (L)	265	6. dependable public services	229
7. friendship	175	7. material needs	224	7. honesty	223
8. positive attitude	175	8. wasted resources (L)	207	8. social responsibility	175
9. humour/fun	158	9. gender discrimination (L)	196	9. human rights	163
10. adaptability	155	10. blame (L)	177	10. poverty reduction	160

Figure 4.3: Values plot for Iceland (2008)

There were eight potentially limiting values in the current culture of Iceland suggesting a significant lack of social cohesion. There were no matching values between the personal values and the current culture and between the current culture and desired culture. There were four matching values between the personal values and desired culture values—accountability, family, financial stability and honesty.

Table 4.4: Value jumps for Iceland (2008)

Values	Current culture votes	Desired culture votes	Value jump
Accountability	10	352	342
Employment opportunities	51	281	230
Financial stability	38	250	212
Honesty	14	223	209
Family	105	308	203
Dependable public services	37	229	192
Optimism	48	233	185
Poverty reduction	13	160	147

It was clear from the value jumps table that the lack of social cohesion in Iceland was due to issues of accountability and honesty, as well as economic concerns (employment opportunities, financial stability and poverty reduction).

UAE assessment

Figure 4.4 shows the results of the National Values Assessment for the UAE carried out in 2012. More than four thousand people participated in this statistically valid survey. Table 4.4 shows the value jumps for the UAE.

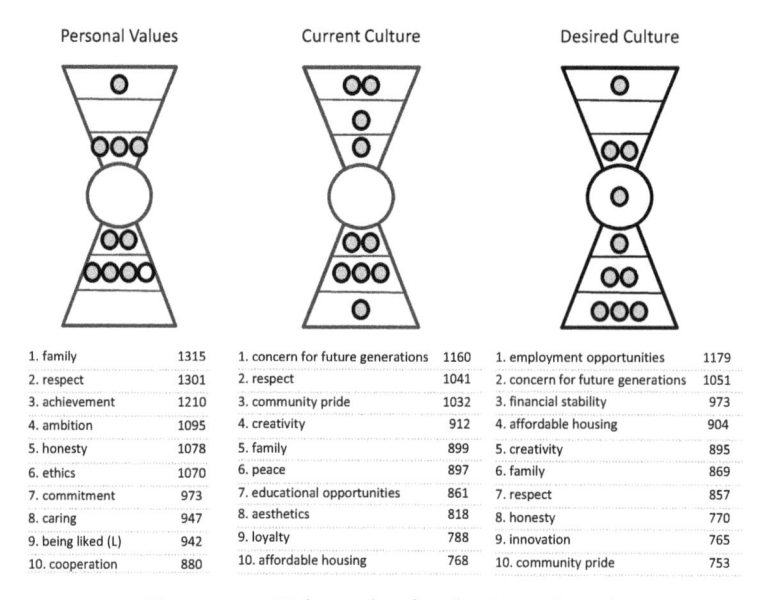

Personal Values		Current Culture		Desired Culture	
1. family	1315	1. concern for future generations	1160	1. employment opportunities	1179
2. respect	1301	2. respect	1041	2. concern for future generations	1051
3. achievement	1210	3. community pride	1032	3. financial stability	973
4. ambition	1095	4. creativity	912	4. affordable housing	904
5. honesty	1078	5. family	899	5. creativity	895
6. ethics	1070	6. peace	897	6. family	869
7. commitment	973	7. educational opportunities	861	7. respect	857
8. caring	947	8. aesthetics	818	8. honesty	770
9. being liked (L)	942	9. loyalty	788	9. innovation	765
10. cooperation	880	10. affordable housing	768	10. community pride	753

Figure 4.4: Values plot for the UAE (2012)

There were no potentially limiting values in the current culture. There were two matching personal and current culture values: family and respect. There were six matching current and desired culture values: concern for future generations, respect, community pride, creativity, family and affordable housing. There were three matching personal and desired culture values: family, respect and honesty. The high number of current and desired culture matches and the lack of potentially limiting values in the current culture suggested a high degree of social cohesion.

Table 4.5: Value jumps for the UAE (2012)

Values	Current culture votes	Desired culture votes	Value jump
Employment opportunities	527	1179	652
Poverty reduction	290	567	277
Effective healthcare	485	740	255
Equality	307	554	247
Transparency	270	503	233
Financial stability	746	973	227
Values awareness	293	498	205
Self-reliance	367	559	192
Accountability	422	612	190
Nature conservancy	433	622	189

It is clear from the values jumps that the most significant issue in the UAE at that time was unemployment. The people of UAE also wanted to see more focus on poverty reduction and effective healthcare. There was also a significant focus on social issues such as equality, transparency and values awareness.

Conclusions

The insight that I had, that social cohesion in a nation is linked to the ability of citizens to get their needs met at the collective stage of psychological development (worldview) they are at, was a significant learning for me. Using this insight, I re-evaluated the results of the National Values Assessments we had carried out in 25 nations. I discovered that I could classify the results into five categories.

- Nations where societal conditions are stable.
- Nations where societal conditions are stable but getting worse.
- Nations where a large proportion of the population desired an upward shift in worldview.
- Nations where a large proportion of the population desired a downward shift in worldview.

- Nations were the leader is proposing a downward shift in worldview, but a large part of the population want to maintain the current worldview.

Nations where societal conditions are stable

The review of the results of the National Values Assessments showed eight nations that fell into this category at the time we carried out their surveys. These were nations with a Cultural Entropy score of less than 40%—Australia (39%), Singapore (37%), Kingdom of Saudi Arabia (34%), Canada (29%), Switzerland (26%), Denmark (21%), the UAE (12%) and Bhutan (4%). Some of these nations were operating from the worldview of People Awareness—Switzerland and Denmark; some were operating from the worldview of World Awareness—Canada, Singapore and Australia; some were operating from State Awareness—Kingdom of Saudi Arabia, the UAE and Bhutan. In all these three latter nations the Cultural Entropy score for males and females was exactly the same or one percentage point different.

Nations where societal conditions are stable but becoming unstable

The review of the results of the National Values Assessments showed three nations that fell into this category (nations with elevated Cultural Entropy scores): Iceland (61%), Finland (49%) and Sweden (from 42% in 2011 to 47% in 2017). All these nations operate from People Awareness but are seeing societal trends that are causing a downward shift towards World Awareness.

Nations where a large proportion of the population desire an upward shift in worldview

The review of the results of the National Values Assessments showed there were nine nations that fell into this category. The people of Belgium want to see an upward shift from World Awareness to People Awareness. The people of France and Italy want to see upward shift from Nation Awareness to World Awareness. The people of Slovakia, Trinidad and Tobago, Latvia and Brazil want to see an upward shift from State Awareness to Nation Awareness. The people of South Africa and Nigeria want to see an upward shift in State Awareness.

Nations where a large proportion of the population desire a downward shift in worldview

The review of the results of the National Values Assessments showed there were two nations that fell into this category: the US and UK. A slim majority of the populations in these nations desire to see a downward shift from World Awareness to Nation Awareness. There are two main causes for these downward shifts.

First, a significant proportion of the populations of these nations got left behind (economically) in the past few decades resulting in increasing levels of inequality and poverty. Second, both nations have been the subject of ongoing terrorist attacks from fundamentalist religious groups. This has caused a retreat from World Awareness (liberalism) to Nation Awareness (nationalism).

Nations where the leader is promoting a downward shift in worldview

The review of the results of the National Values Assessments showed there were two nations that fell into this category: Venezuela and Turkey. The leaders of Venezuela and Turkey are seeking more control and power: they are attempting to force their nations into a deeper (more radical) form of State Awareness.

I think it is important to point out that I could only make the above comments because we have carried out National Values Assessments in these countries.

Longitudinal monitoring of changes in the social cohesion of nations

To date, we only have two examples of nations where we have carried National Values Assessments over a period of years: France and Sweden.

In both cases, private sponsors, who were interested in helping to build a values-driven nation, financed these values assessments.

France

Table 4.6 shows the Cultural Entropy scores for France (2012 – 2016)

Table 4.6: Cultural Entropy scores for France (2012 – 2016)

Year	2012	2013	2014	2015	2016
Cultural Entropy	57%	65%	65%	61%	65%

Comments on the Cultural Entropy scores for France

The first National Values Assessment in France was undertaken in 2012 while President Sarkozy was still in office. The cultural entropy score was 57%. There was unrest because people had become angry with Sarkozy: he wasn't meeting their needs, and later that year they voted him out of office. There was a lot of hope when the Socialist François Hollande was elected: there was an expectation that employment would grow. However, after one year in office, nothing had changed. The economic indicators had not improved, and the turmoil in Hollande's personal life was creating a public distraction. The French people felt deceived and let down. The Cultural Entropy score increased to 65% in 2013 and stayed there in the following year.

Strangely, the "Charlie Hebdo" terrorist attack in 2015, which killed 12 people, caused the level of Cultural Entropy to drop to 61% (an increase in social cohesion). The emotional outpouring caused by this attack convinced people more than ever to embrace the value of freedom of speech (the Charlie Hebdo publication was a bastion of free speech) and the importance of the separation of religion and state. The French people came together in solidarity against the terrorists.

The following year the values assessment took place within days of the terrorist attack in Nice which killed 85 people. This event increased the public perception of terrorism: social cohesion went down, and the Cultural Entropy score went back to 65%.

Comments on the value jumps for France

Two of the biggest value jumps in France were remarkably consistent. Government efficiency and justice appeared every year from 2012 to 2016. Employment opportunities occurred in four out of the five years.

The Hollande government was plagued by inefficiency. Consequently year after year "government efficiency" became the number one values jump. The great hopes for more employment and a more efficient justice system did not happen (it takes many years to resolve a law suit in France). The inefficiency in the justice system creates the impression that if you can afford to retain a good lawyer, you can evade punishment.

A failure to live up to the value of honesty, which is one of the top personal values of the French, led to the demise of the favourite presidential candidate François Fillon in 2017. This opened the door for Emmanuel Macron who became the new President in 2017. Once again there is great hope that France will change. Let's see what happens to the National Values Assessment results next year. It is interesting to note, because of the terrorist troubles, that "peace" became one of the top five value jumps in 2016.

Sweden

Table 4.7 shows the Cultural Entropy scores for Sweden (2009 – 2017).[43]

Table 4.7: Cultural Entropy scores for Sweden (2009 – 2017)

Year	2009	2010	2011	2012
Cultural Entropy	31%	34%	42%	43%
Year	**2013**	**2014**	**2016**	**2017**
Cultural Entropy	47%	43%	47%	46%

Comments on the Cultural Entropy scores for Sweden

The Cultural Entropy scores for Sweden rose from 31% in 2009 and 34% in 2010 to 47% in 2016 and 47% in 2017, indicating that social cohesion

---

[43] A National Values Assessment was not carried out in 2015.

decreased over this seven-year period. In the first part of this period, the Global Economic meltdown, which occurred in 2008 – 2009, had a significant impact on the economy of Sweden. This raised anxieties about financial security and unemployment, which in turn led to an increase in potentially limiting values such as insecurity about the future, materialistic, blame and short-term focus.

In the second of this part of this period, there was a large intake of foreign migrants. This led to an increase in anxiety about the future which in turn led to an increase in potentially limiting values such as violence and crime, conflict and aggression and hate. Because of these two events—the global economic meltdown and the influx of refugees—the people of Sweden are finding it more difficult to live in People Awareness, and the level of social cohesion is going down.

Comments on the value jumps for Sweden

The biggest value jumps in Sweden are remarkably consistent. Employment opportunities, concern for future generations and financial stability were in the top five value jumps every year. Caring for the elderly occurred in six out of the eight years. Effective health care has shown up in the top five desired culture values in the last six years.

This consistency in value jumps we believe in large part is because the leaders in Sweden are out of touch with the needs of their people. Social conditions are changing, but the policies and attitudes of the politicians are not. The one area that has received some attention is effective health care probably because this issue has consistently received a lot of press coverage over the past few years.

Conclusions

What we see in the two longitudinal case studies is the possibility of creating a values dashboard for monitoring the cultural health of a nation. This is exactly what we do in organizations. The data on values provides lead indicators on the level of internal cohesion and the key issues which need to be addressed in organizational, community and national cultures. When you break down the data by demographics—age, gender, ethnicity, religion, social status, etc.—one can immediately see, comparing year on year results, where the social pressure points are building up and take actions to alleviate these tensions before they spill over into unrest.

The evolution of human consciousness depends on the leaders

Communities and nations grow and develop in the same way as individuals, by expanding the level of identity and awareness (of their citizens). This can only happen if the leaders create the conditions that support citizens in meeting their needs at the stage of psychological development they are at. Only when people can master their needs, are they able to progress to the next stage of development. This progression leads to the adoption of a higher order worldview.

If the people of a particular community (ethnic group) are content operating at the collective stage of development (worldview) they are at, the Government should not pressure them to change their way of life. On the contrary, Governments should find ways to support them.

This is why it is important to map the values of all groups and communities (ethnicity, age, gender, religion) on a regular basis to identify the group's or community's most important needs. If Governments do not support communities in meeting their needs, or if certain groups get left behind economically, this will cause those people to experience distress and suffering. This, in turn, will lead to a decrease in social cohesion and an increase in Cultural Entropy.

The first point—supporting people in living the way of life they choose—is amply illustrated by the demise of what is known as the people of the First Nations. For decades, successive US, Canadian, Australian and to a certain extent New Zealand Governments, tried to get their indigenous people to accept a worldview that was foreign them. They were living in Clan Awareness or Tribe Awareness, but the Governments tried to force them to live in Nation or World Awareness. The impact on the people of these communities was disastrous: their mental and physical health deteriorated considerably.

In one Aborigine community in North Queensland known as Napranam, this situation has been reversed. A community values assessment in 2011 recorded a Cultural Entropy score of 33%. In June 2013, a repeat assessment recorded a Cultural Entropy score of just 9%. Social cohesion was increased by 24 points in just over two years. Community engagement was the top desired culture value in 2011, and by 2013 it had become the top current culture value. Allowing the people of Napranam to become responsible and accountable for their futures and finding the funds to support them in meeting their needs completely changed the community. Since 2011, there has been a 40% increase in community infrastructure, a 60% increase in employment and an 80% decrease in adult domestic violence. This is an example of how indigenous leaders came together with corporate and government interests to share skills and knowledge and thereby create real change.[44],[45]

The second point—when groups of people get left behind due to rising levels of inequality—is amply illustrated by the recent socio-political trends in the UK and US. If we take the UK, for example, successive governments in the recent years have ignored and consequently failed to meet the needs of more than half of the UK's citizens. This is what led to the Brexit vote in 2016, and the demise of the Conservative party in the 2017 general election. These events would never have happened if the government had paid attention to the needs of *all* citizens, not just the elites who were successfully operating from World Awareness, but also the less educated and older people who were operating from Nation Awareness.

In the UK National Values Assessment[46] sponsored and carried out by the Barrett Values Centre in 2012, the value priorities (largest value jumps) were honesty, caring for the disadvantaged, affordable housing, employment opportunities, accountability, caring for the elderly and dependable public services. Governments since that time paid little attention to these needs. In fact, they did just the opposite. Year after year they cut the budgets for welfare and public services.

The same dynamic occurred in the US in 2016. The underprivileged majority resonated with Donald Trump because he spoke their language—the language of Nation Awareness. Hilary Clinton, on the other hand, spoke the language of World Awareness. The high Cultural Entropy scores we measured in the US in 2009 and 2011 were signs that all was not well in

---

[44] Banksia Sustainability Awards at http://bit.ly/2rF6FCA
[45] Case Study: Napranum Aboriginal Shire at http://bit.ly/2sNrUDy
[46] UK National Values Assessment at http://bit.ly/2sEapp6

the nation. As in the UK, we suspected it was due to a lack of social cohesion caused by the issue of inequality.

The main lesson to be drawn from these experiences is that we must pay attention to the needs of all the groups and communities that make up a nation, not just the needs of the elites. The needs of everyone must be considered, including people of different ethnic backgrounds, religious faiths, and socio-economic groupings. This is much easier to do in nations with homogenous populations, such as the Scandinavian nations, than in nations which are ethnically diverse.

However, the longitudinal surveys we have done in Sweden show that when you attempt to integrate people of different ethnic origins (worldviews) into a homogenous culture, you stand the risk of disrupting the internal cohesion of the nation.

I am not arguing that nations operating from Nation Awareness or World Awareness should not provide a haven for refugees from different ethnic backgrounds—people with different worldviews—what I am arguing is that this should be done with a thorough understanding of the differences between the worldviews of the immigrants and the worldviews that exist in the host nation. It can take several generations for the families of immigrants to adopt the worldview of their host nation.

Integrating people of different ethnicities into nations operating from the worldview of Nation Awareness will always prove to be difficult because in this worldview people who look different, speak a foreign language or belong to a different faith are discriminated against. Furthermore, it is completely pointless trying to integrate refugees into nations operating from State Awareness—they will suffer intense discrimination. The most welcoming environment for refugees will always be nations operating from People Awareness. Why? Because this worldview is more inclusive and accepting of diversity than all the other worldviews.

Richard Barrett

Epilogue

HERE IS A BRIEF SUMMARY of the main points of the book.

Whatever you need is what you value, and what you value is the satisfaction of the needs of the stage of psychological development you are at and the unmet needs of the stages of psychological development you have passed through that you have not yet mastered. As you make progress mastering the needs of each stage of psychological development you become less focused on self and more focused on others.

When you reach the individuating stage of psychological development, you stop using your beliefs for making decisions and start using your values. As you reach the higher stages of psychological development, you realize that at the deepest level of your being we all share the same values.

To be successful in business, or running any organization, you must support your employees in meeting their needs at the stages of psychological development they are at, and you must also help them to resolve their unmet needs from previous stages of development. This means supporting them in their personal transformation.

Personal transformation is particularly important for supervisors, managers and leaders because who they are, and how they turn up at work, defines the culture of an organization. Organizations don't transform. People do. Therefore, if you want to change the culture of your organization you must either change your leaders or your leaders must change. To this end, it is vitally important that you monitor the culture of your organization on a regular basis.

Everyone grows in stages (of psychological development), operates at levels of consciousness and lives inside a worldview which reflects the collective stage of psychological development that the community or nation they were born into (and live in) has reached.

The evolution of worldviews of communities and nations mirrors the evolution of the individual stages of psychological development. In other words, the values component at each stage of our collective psychological development is a direct reflection of the values component of each stage of our individual psychological development.

The evolution of human consciousness depends on the leaders of every community and nation supporting their citizens in meeting the needs they have at the stage of psychological development they have reached; not just the elites, but everyone, including the disadvantaged, minorities and the poor.

Regular monitoring of the culture, as perceived by different groups or communities within a nation—gender, age, ethnicity, and so on—is not just important for maintaining the internal cohesion of a nation, it is also important for making the evolution of human consciousness, conscious.

Annex 1

The formation of Hitler's personality

AS PART OF THE AMERICAN war effort, Dr. Henry A. Murray [47] carried out a psychoanalytical study of Hitler in October 1943. Murray's analysis, of which extracts appear in the following paragraphs, can be found at Cornell University's Law Library's web site. The full text, which comprises more than 150 pages, provides many more details.

Hitler was born in Austria in 1889. He was the fourth of six children. His father, an illegitimate child, was a tyrant. He looked on Adolf as a weakling and a good-for-nothing, handing out frequent physical punishments. Consequently, Hitler was afraid of his father. He was timid and submissive in his presence, but unruly and defiant otherwise. In *Mein Kampf*[48], Hitler speaks of old men in a derogatory and contemptuous manner, suggestive of his sentiments for his father. His mother was very compliant towards his father, but she was also devoted to Adolf, catering to all his whims. Hitler loved his mother and hated his father.

Hitler was a frail child. He had a low tolerance for frustration. His father was unusually severe and his mother inordinately lenient. As a result, he developed no steady and consistent character. He alternated between subservience and unruliness. He also resisted his father's wishes through

---

[47] Dr. Henry Murray was the Director of the Harvard Psychological Clinic during the Second World War and served in the Office of Strategic Services (OSS). The OSS was a forerunner of the Central Intelligence Agency (CIA).

[48] *Mein Kampf* is a book written by Adolf Hitler. It combines elements of autobiography with an exposition of his political ideology. Volume 1 was published in 1925 and Volume 2 was published a year later.

passivity or illness. In this manner, he learned how to manipulate people to his will.

Hitler was constantly thwarted by his father. He wanted to attend a classical high school and become an artist. His father wanted him to follow in his footsteps and become an Austrian custom's official. He sent Hitler to a technical high school. Hitler rebelled against this decision and failed his first year, hoping that once his father saw what little progress he was making he would let him follow his dream. That was not to be. His father was unrelenting in wanting to mold his child's future, which made Hitler even more bitter and rebellious. After his father died, Hitler's behaviour became so bad that he was asked to leave the technical high school without completing his studies.

He fell back on his dream to be an artist, but this fell short when he was rejected by the Academy of Fine Arts. He was recommended to study architecture, but his poor school record was against him. He did not have the academic credentials needed from his technical high school to attend the architectural school. He tried to sell his paintings (copies of postcards) to merchants and tourists. He eventually ran out of money and lived for a time in a shelter for the homeless in Vienna. All of this must have been frustrating for him, and in some ways confirmed his father's disappointment in his son.

German nationalism became an obsession for Hitler; it was a way to rebel against his father, who had proudly served the Austrian government. Hitler's declaration that he demanded nothing but sacrifices from his adherents is reminiscent of the father's attitude towards his wife and children. To the extent that he emulated his father, he disrespected and denied his mother. His strong dependent attachment to her was, for him, a humiliating sign of his incapacity to take care of himself. Hence he was forced to belittle the relationship with his mother and devalue women.

Hitler's fanatical sentiments against mixed marriage, impure blood, the lower classes, and the Jewish race, were a repudiation of his past. His forbearers came from a region in which the blood of many different nationalities had mixed for generations. His father was illegitimate, and his grandfather may have been a Viennese Jew. His father begot at least one child out of marriage. Hitler's older half-sister ran a restaurant for Jewish students. Hitler's younger sister was the mistress of a Jew for a period.

Most of Hitler's relatives were either feeble-minded, ignorant, illiterate or mentally retarded. The person he pretended to be was the exact opposite of all this, suggesting compensating feelings of inferiority and self-contempt. Hitler never visited his familial home or communicated with his relatives in over thirty years. Although born an Austrian, Hitler identified with Germany. He glorified the history of Germany.

The German Culture

Hitler seized power in 1933 and consolidated his position as a dictator by fanning the flames of nationalism among the German people. The general feeling in Germany at that time was of great despondency. There was civil unrest, attributed to Marxist groups, growing hyperinflation caused by the Great Depression, and a sense of national shame, embarrassment and resentment resulting from the reparations that Germany had to pay to other European countries as a result of the First World War and the Treaty of Versailles[49].

As the head of the Nazi Party, Hitler promised strong authoritarian government, civic peace, radical improvements in the economy, and most importantly, restored national pride. Also in the name of national unity and solidarity, the Nazi Party proposed racial cleansing, partly implemented through the active suppression of Jews and Marxists. Along with this national renewal, the party promised rearmament, repudiation of reparations and reclamation of territory lost in the Treaty of Versailles.

Hitler's appeal to the German people was the strong firm control he brought to the country at a time of great economic and political turmoil. His focus on the restoration of pride to the "motherland" made the German people feel good. They wanted to be respected, stand tall again, and leave the shame and embarrassment of the past behind. The ego of the nation needed healing and Hitler was seen as the man who could restore their pride.

Unfortunately, Hitler's own need for healing was far greater than the nation's. The German nation became the instrument by which he would attempt to restore his battered ego. As always with ego deficiencies, such as not having enough, not being loved enough, and not being respected

---

[49] The Treaty of Versailles was one of the peace treaties signed at the end of the First World War. The treaty required Germany to accept responsibility for causing the war, to disarm, make substantial territorial concessions and pay heavy reparations to certain countries.

enough, enough is never enough. Once the fears of the ego get hardwired into the subconscious mind, they are always present, lurking in the background, constantly waiting to be fed. Fears as significant as Hitler's can only be released through intense psychological work. Based on the above, we can state that Hitler's worldview was strongly influenced by his personal belief system. The worldview he adopted led to the deaths of over 60 million people, which at that time represented 3% of the world population.

Annex 2

The formation of Gandhi's personality

IN CONTRAST TO HITLER, WHOSE worldview was strongly influenced by his personal belief system, I would like to discuss Mohandas Gandhi's worldview, which was strongly influenced by his cosmological belief system. Since I do not have the benefit of an analysis of Gandhi's personality, similar to Murray's analysis of Hitler available for study, I have used Gandhi's autobiography[50] to piece together the factors that I believe influenced his early development and his subsequent worldview.

Gandhi, who is recognized as the leader of the Indian Independence movement, was born in Porbandar in the Bombay region in 1869. His father was a high official in the state government, and several of his close relatives had held high ranking positions in various Indian states. His father was truthful, brave and generous, but even though he was short-tempered, he never raised a hand in punishment to any of his children. He was regarded as incorruptible and earned the respect of others for his strict impartiality within his family, as well as outside. Gandhi describes his mother as a Saint. She was deeply religious, well informed on all matters and had strong common sense. Unlike Hitler, Gandhi was loved and well treated by his parents. Consequently, he was devoted and respectful to them and willingly acceded to their wish that he become a barrister.

While studying law in England, he became interested in religious thought. For him, this was not about following a particular religion; it

---

[50] M.K. Gandhi, *Gandhi: An Autobiography or The Story of My Experiments with Truth* (Penguin Books: London), 2008 (first published in two volumes in 1927 and 1929).

was about self-realization, self-knowledge and personal growth. He had a highly developed sense of self-witnessing[51], which he used to analyze his motives for everything he did. He considered every project in his life to be an experiment in Truth.

With this background of integrity on his father's side and saintliness on his mother's side, it is not surprising that these early influences on Gandhi led him to have compassion for all sentient beings, vegetarianism, fasting for self-purification and mutual tolerance among people of different creeds. He developed an early identification with Truth and Love. Even as a young child he could not tell a lie. His need to live in alignment with the principle of Truth was so strong, that whenever he felt he was not living to the highest standards possible, he would be extremely hard on himself. He found it hard to forgive himself, but easy to be forgiving of others.

What is noticeable about Gandhi's childhood is that all his deficiency needs were met. He felt safe and secure; he felt loved by his parents and family; he was respected by those around him. Thus, unlike Hitler, who lived out his life trying to find the love and recognition that was denied him as a child, by the time Gandhi reached adulthood he was ready for individuation and self-actualization. That is not to say that Gandhi was perfect; in his own eyes, he never was. But he had a fully-developed capacity for continuous learning, both about himself and the world around him—a true sign of a seeker of truth.

At the end of his biography, Gandhi states:

"The path of self-purification is hard and steep. To attain perfect purity one has to become passion-free, in thought, speech and action; to rise above the opposing currents of love and hatred, attachment and repulsion. To conquer the subtle passions seems to me to be far harder than the physical conquest of the world by force of arms. I have had experiences of the dormant passions lying within me. The knowledge of them has made me feel humiliated though not defeated. The experiences and experiments [in Truth] have sustained me and given me great joy. But I know that I have still before me a difficult path to traverse. I must reduce myself to zero. For as long as a

---

[51] Self-witnessing is a term I use in the *New Leadership Paradigm* to describe an individual's ability to stand back from his or her experiences and observe his or her thoughts, feelings and emotions.

man does not of his own free will put himself last among his fellow creatures, there is no salvation for him. Ahimsa (doing no harm/non-violence) is the farthest limit of humility."

The Indian Culture

Gandhi's appeal to the people of India was that he was one of the few Indian leaders who were able to successfully gain concessions from the ruling British Raj. He was seen as a saviour in the Indian Independence movement. His weapons in this struggle were non-cooperation, non-violence and peaceful resistance. He later extended his non-violence platform to include the boycott of all foreign-made goods, especially British goods.

Non-cooperation enjoyed widespread appeal and success, increasing the level of excitement and participation from all strata of Indian society. Gandhi's gift was that he was able to unite the people of India—the members of all castes and all religions. However, once freedom was in sight, this unity quickly evaporated, and the return to division and hierarchy, which is an integral part of Indian culture, was quick to re-establish.[52]

Although very popular among the people, Gandhi was not enamoured with politics. His fight was for the people of India and not for himself. He was a reluctant campaigner, called into service for the people by India's leading politicians. His preference was to be at home in his Ashram.

---

[52] It is interesting to note that social cohesion is more easily achieved when the people of a nation experience a common external threat. This mechanism enabled Winston Churchill to galvanise the efforts of Great Britain against the Germans in the Second World War. As soon as the war was over, Churchill was cast aside as the leader of the country.

INDEX

A

The ability to bond 49, 51
The ability to cooperate 49, 51
Abraham Maslow xxii, xxiii, 5
Adaptability 29, 49, 50, 51
Arab Spring 5
Autonomy 6, 7, 22, 26, 27, 29, 31, 35, 38, 45, 77

B

Barrett Values Centre iii, v, x, xx, xxiii, 39, 40, 47, 86, 98
Beliefs 4, 5, 9, 11, 14, 16, 17, 28, 30, 31, 36, 40, 50, 51, 60, 75, 77, 78, 79, 82, 101, 106, 107
Björn Larsson xx
Blame 6, 7, 18, 44, 96
Brexit 98
Buddhism xxi, 8
Business School of Lausanne 84

C

Charlie Hebdo 94
Clan awareness 55, 56, 57, 58, 59, 60, 61, 97
Clare Graves 54
Complexity 49, 51, 52, 82
Conforming 18, 19, 20, 24, 26, 28, 29, 30, 56, 57, 62
Conscience 1, 9
Continuous learning 4, 49, 50, 51, 108
Cosmology 58, 59, 61, 62, 65, 68, 72, 73, 75, 76, 79
Cultural capital 37, 39
Cultural entropy x, 42, 43, 45, 47, 86, 87, 88, 92, 94, 95, 97, 98
Cultural Transformation Tools x, xxii, 40, 86
Cultural Values Assessment 40, 41, 47, 87

D

Differentiating 20, 22, 25, 26, 27, 29, 31, 56, 57, 65, 66, 70, 73
Donald Trump 98

E

Earth awareness 54, 55, 56, 57, 80, 81
Ego viii, 1, 6, 8, 14, 15, 17, 18, 19, 22, 32, 34, 35, 62, 63, 64, 65, 67, 74, 76, 79, 80, 105, 106
Emotional intelligence 20, 24
Emotions 14, 108
Employee viii, xxi, 37, 38, 39, 40, 41, 43, 44, 45, 47, 49, 101
Ethics 1, 9
Evolutionary Dynamics 55
Evolutionary leader 37, 49, 51

Evolution of worldviews 82, 102

F

Feelings 2, 4, 8, 16, 17, 18, 19, 22, 23, 24, 25, 26, 27, 31, 33, 76, 105, 108
Foresight Group xx, 57
France 72, 85, 86, 87, 92, 94, 95
François Fillon 95
François Hollande 94
Freedom 5, 6, 7, 8, 22, 23, 26, 27, 29, 31, 35, 38, 55, 57, 69, 74, 77, 94, 109
Full-spectrum consciousness x, 12, 34

G

Gandhi 107, 108, 109
GAPFRAME 84
GCI 83, 84, 85
Global Consciousness Indicator xx, 83, 84, 85

H

Happiness indicator 83
Hatred 7, 108
High-performance organization xx, 38, 41, 42, 44, 45, 46
Hitler 65, 103, 104, 105, 106, 107, 108
Humanity awareness 55, 56, 57, 77, 78, 79, 80

I

Iceland Assessment 88
Individuating 5, 6, 22, 23, 24, 26, 27, 28, 29, 36, 56, 57, 76, 77, 101
Integrating 19, 24, 25, 26, 27, 29, 56, 57, 72, 73, 99
Integrity 1, 10, 29, 31, 47, 108
Internal cohesion consciousness 32

J

Jealousy 7, 29

L

Liberalism 93
Liberating the Corporate Soul viii, xxii
Longitudinal monitoring 93
Love, Fear and the Destiny of Nations viii, 78
Low-performance organization 41, 42, 43

M

Making a difference consciousness 33
Monitoring 37, 46, 47, 53, 93, 96, 102
Morals 1, 3, 9, 10, 12, 67
Moral values 1, 9

N

Napranam 97, 98
Nationalism 93, 104, 105
National Values Assessment 53, 86, 88, 90, 91, 92, 93, 94, 95, 98
Nation awareness 55, 56, 57, 64, 67, 68, 69, 70, 71, 73, 74, 75, 76, 77, 78, 85, 87, 92, 93, 98, 99
Nedbank 46, 47
Needs ii, iii, iv, xx, xxii, 4, 5, 6, 7, 8, 11, 13, 14, 15, 16, 17, 18, 19, 20, 21, 22, 23, 24, 25, 26, 27, 28, 30, 31, 32, 33, 34, 35, 36, 37, 38, 39, 41, 44, 46, 49, 50, 52, 53, 54, 65, 66, 67, 70, 76, 77, 78, 81, 86, 91, 94, 96, 97, 98, 99, 101, 102, 105, 108
The New Leadership Paradigm viii, 47, 49, 50, 108
A New Psychology of Human Well-Being viii, 14, 79

O

Organizational values 7

P

People awareness 55, 56, 57, 72, 74, 75, 76, 77, 78, 79, 80, 85, 87, 88, 92, 96, 99
Personal values 2, 3, 12, 13, 41, 44, 89, 95
Personal Values Assessment 2, 3, 12, 13
Positive values 6, 28, 41, 48
Potentially limiting values 6, 7, 28, 29, 41, 42, 43, 44, 48, 89, 90, 96
Psychological development x, xx, 15, 22, 26, 28, 34, 37, 53, 54, 56, 57, 58, 60, 62, 65, 66, 70, 73, 74, 76, 77, 78, 79, 82, 86, 91, 97, 101, 102

R

Relationship consciousness 30
Relationship values 7, 8, 44
The Rise of the Meaningful Economy xx, 57

S

Self-actualizing 23, 24, 25, 26, 27, 29, 56, 57, 76, 79
Self-esteem consciousness 31
Service consciousness 33, 41
Serving 6, 22, 25, 26, 27, 29, 56, 57
Seven Levels of Consciousness iv, v, x, xxii, xxiii, 3, 12, 28, 30, 41, 54, 83
Seven Stages of Development 28
Social Cohesion 53, 86, 88, 89, 90, 91, 93, 94, 96, 97, 98, 99, 109
Social integration 75, 82
Societal values 7

Soul ii, vi, viii, xxi, xxii, 2, 8, 9, 10, 14, 15, 16, 17, 18, 20, 22, 23, 24, 25, 26, 31, 32, 33, 34, 35, 36, 59, 60, 72, 73, 75, 79, 80, 81, 82
Spiral Dynamics 54
Stages of psychological development x, xx, 15, 26, 28, 53, 54, 56, 57, 58, 78, 101, 102
State awareness 55, 56, 57, 62, 63, 64, 65, 66, 67, 68, 74, 85, 87, 88, 92, 93, 99
Survival consciousness 30, 41
Surviving 8, 16, 18, 26, 28, 30, 56, 57, 60
Sweden ii, xix, 85, 86, 87, 92, 94, 95, 96, 99

T

Tom Boardman 46
Transformation consciousness 31, 41
Tribe awareness 55, 56, 57, 60, 61, 62, 81, 85, 97

U

UAE Assessment 90
Unity awareness 55, 56, 57, 80, 81, 82
Universal values 11, 34
Unskilled worker 38
UN sustainable development goals 81, 84

V

Value jumps 43, 44, 45, 46, 89, 90, 91, 95, 96, 98
Value priorities 11, 13, 15, 28, 78, 98
Values-based decision-making 1, 4, 5, 10, 36
The Values-driven Organization viii, 39, 47, 49
Values of humanity 2, 49
Vedic Philosophy xxii, xxiii

Virtues 1, 8, 9
VUCA 50

W

Winston Churchill 109
World awareness 55, 56, 57, 64, 70, 71,
    72, 73, 74, 75, 76, 85, 87, 92, 93,
    97, 98, 99
World Bank xxi, xxii, xxiii
Worldviews i, 8, 34, 38, 53, 54, 55, 56,
    57, 58, 59, 60, 61, 62, 63, 64, 65,
    66, 67, 68, 69, 70, 71, 72, 73, 74,
    75, 76, 77, 78, 79, 80, 81, 82, 85,
    86, 87, 88, 91, 92, 93, 97, 99, 101,
    102, 106, 107

Y

Yang 8
Yin 8